Skyscrapers of New York

Skyscrapers of New York

Seth Gopin

2012

MI

New York

Library of Congress Control Number: 2012902807
ISBN: 978-0-9838909-1-1

No part of the contents of this book may be reproduced, stored in a retrieval system, or transmitted in any form or by any means, electronic, mechanical, photocopying, recording, or otherwise, without the express written permission of Seth Gopin and Metro Insights, LLC.

© 2011 by Metro Insights, LLC
All rights reserved. First edition 2011.
Second edition 2012.

Printed and bound by Oceanic Graphic Printing, China

Metro Insights, LLC
12 West 72nd Street, 2C
New York, NY 10023

www.metroinsights.com

Contents

Introduction	7
Acknowledgments	8
Manhattan's Crowning Glories	11
The Old New York Times Building	23
Bayard-Condict Building	27
Flatiron Building	29
Metropolitan Life Tower	33
Woolworth Building	37
Equitable Building	41
American Radiator Building	43
Chrysler Building	47
Empire State Building	51
Rockefeller Center	55
Lever House	65
Seagram Building	69
Pan Am Building	73
World Trade Center	77
American Telephone & Telegraph Building	81
Condé Nast Building	85
Westin New York at Times Square	89
Time Warner Center	93
Hearst Tower	95
New York Times Building	99
New York by Gehry	101
Maps	
Lower Manhattan	103
Madison Square	105
Midtown Manhattan	107
Bibliography	109

INTRODUCTION

The origin of this book can be traced back twenty years to the time when I was a young dean at Rutgers University in New Jersey. A colleague was hosting the biannual gathering of the International Society of Historical Linguists on the New Brunswick campus, and renowned scholars were flying in from all parts of the world to attend. As everyone wanted to go to New York during their one free afternoon, I suggested putting together a tour of the city's skyscrapers. The chair of the conference questioned the wisdom of this proposal: "They are just buildings. What can be interesting about skyscrapers?" I boldly replied, "No, skyscrapers represent everything that is good about America especially New York. Besides, it will get the visitors all around the city." With his reluctant approval, I delved into learning about the many buildings for an afternoon bus tour.

The day of the tour arrived, a glorious, sunny day, and the bus filled up with senior linguists from the four corners of the globe. Some were skeptical that they would learn anything of note about the buildings but, they reasoned, at least they would see New York. By the end of the tour, my group of reluctant academics was 100% converted to the merits of New York's skyscrapers. Over a wonderful Chinese banquet we argued about the changing styles of the buildings, about the propriety of a "cathedral of commerce," and about the future of such buildings. I knew then that looking at buildings from an art historical perspective was both intellectually rewarding as well as fun.

In the years between that first tour in 1989 and the writing of this book, I have had the pleasure of discussing New York skyscrapers with a generation of Rutgers undergraduates, VIPs from all around the world, and with passengers aboard the Cunard Line. For me, one pleasure in talking about New York's skyscrapers is that no lecture or tour is the same; there is always something new to discuss and see. Students and audience members always bring fresh insights and ideas.

Much has changed since the 1990s, and skyscrapers have evolved significantly. Post-Modernism was a brand-new style, super tall buildings outside of the United States were rare, and no one believed that a skyscraper could be considered environmentally friendly. Most importantly, after the fall of the Twin Towers on September 11, 2001, the skyscraper has loomed large in the collective zeitgeist of people all over the world. Skyscrapers are no longer just office buildings but icons of culture and commerce, emblems of civic and national pride.

Seth Gopin
New York City
July 4, 2011

Facing page, Crowns of Cass Gilbert's Woolworth Building and *New York by Gehry*. Above, Cook + Fowle, Bank of America Tower, completed 2009, the second largest building in New York City.

ACKNOWLEDGMENTS

Over the last thirty years I have been extremely fortunate to have as mentor, colleague, friend, and partner, Dr. Martin Eidelberg. From my first day in his 1976 *Introduction to Art History* course to his insightful comments and multiple edits on the many drafts of this manuscript, he has taught me what art and architecture are all about. Through encouragement, goading, nudging, and sometimes a "kindly" shove, Martin made me think about the complexities of skyscrapers in New York and around the world. For everything, he has my heartfelt thanks.

I have been lucky enough to be a Wertheim Study writer-in-residence in the New York Public Library's Stephen A. Schwarzman Building at 42nd Street, one of the world's best research libraries. Jay Barksdale, who oversees this program, has been so helpful in advancing my project. Clayton C. Kirking, Chief of Art Information Resources, and his entire staff went out of their way to help me. Lillian 'Lulu' Santamaria's creative spirit greatly improved this new edition.

At Rutgers University where I worked and taught for twenty-seven years, a generation of Rutgers honors students helped me develop a New York skyscraper tour, and in the past few years, the Rutgers Club of New York has been supportive and allowed me to hone my skills by speaking to their members. Over my three decades at Rutgers, I had the pleasure to work with very talented people. In the Study Abroad Office, Brigid Brown and Steve Ferst were supportive colleagues and friends who always allowed me to sneak away to work on not only skyscrapers but much more. In Global Programs, Henriette Cohen assisted me for many years and deserves a special thank you.

A few years ago, when I lived in Lewes in East Sussex, my wonderful neighbors on St. Anne's Crescent, Pamela Tudor Craig and Annette and Vincent Hope, helped me shape early versions of this manuscript. Paul and Kathy Myles on Hill Road have become great friends and through Paul's publication on *Tom Paine in Lewes,* I was inspired to launch this project.

For several years, Cunard has allowed me to lecture on their world-class ships—the Queen Mary 2, Queen Victoria, and Queen Elizabeth. On shore, Caroline Mathieson and Tim Wilkin gave me a platform to lecture and advance my ideas. On board, Entertainment Directors Ray Rouse, Amanda Reid, and Paul O'Loughlin were wonderfully supportive of my lectures and work. My tablemates in the Britannia Restaurant over the years have been great critics and fans. The guests aboard the ships, whether first-time visitors to the Big Apple or seasoned New

Lower Manhattan from the deck of Queen Mary 2.

Yorkers, have been the reason why I wanted to do this book. I have enjoyed chatting with them all and thank them for their insightful questions and comments.

Patrick and Marie-José Ramade of Caen and Danielle Decadi of Rennes accompanied me on an unforgettable skyscraper tour in New York City one glorious afternoon and we talked about architecture and tall buildings from a European viewpoint. Merci mille fois.

Singapore, the home of some of the most creative buildings today, was another venue that gave me new insights. Over superb tea and wonderful meals, Beljean Ong, May Teo, Kevin Baraka, and Ai-Lin Chuah discussed architecture and made me welcome in that far-away land.

Andrew Freedman was kind enough to introduce me to Marcus Oberlin, the general manager of the Burj Khalifa in Dubai, the world's tallest building. The deputy facilities manager Niranjan Sam, and Mr. Ahmed went out of their way to welcome us and walked us through the building from the sub-basement to the unfinished 148th floor. Likewise, Louis Nowikas' special tour of the Hearst Tower was extremely edifying. My new appreciation and understanding of how a skyscraper runs comes from them.

Without question my biggest supporter these past few years has been Daniel S. Palmer. Dan, my mentee and friend, embraced the world of skyscrapers, Vanmour, Thomas Paine, and much more. He has read many drafts of this manuscript and helped shape the overall project. Thank you for all of this.

My love of New York comes from my family. My father, Stan, has always told stories about his life in New York in the 1950s that have made me jealous to have missed that vibrant time. Even though my aunt, Vivian Ross, lives in Arizona, she is the consummate New Yorker, with a New Yorker's soul. Both of them were the very first to introduce me to the city. My uncle Leonard Ross, who was a photographer for Bethlehem Steel, stimulated my interest in photography and it is only fitting that his photo of the Chase Manhattan Building under construction serves as the frontispiece for this book. My sister Evan and her husband John helped me from the very beginning of this project and have been a huge support for me. Yaksha, Evan's Tibetan spaniel, has been the mascot of this project from the beginning. As well, my cousins Eve and Tracy and their families in Flagstaff and Seattle have been involved and supportive at different stages in this long process, as has my Ohio family.

My great regret is that my mother, Sondra, did not live long enough to see this publication. She was instrumental in shaping my life as an art historian. I am indebted to her for much of who I am today.

Discussing architecture in Brighton Beach; from left to right, Danielle Decadi, Dan Palmer, Martin Eidelberg, Marie-José Ramade, and Seth Gopin.

Acknowledgments | 9

The changing skylines of New York in 1651, 1902, and 2010.

MANHATTAN'S CROWNING GLORIES

The towering buildings of New York City that the world has come to know and admire are a New York story. Although the origins of the skyscraper can be traced to Chicago, its development happened in New York City. The great buildings were defined by considerable social, economic, and technological forces that are part of the American spirit and express a materialistic as well as a national culture. In the early twentieth century, a series of New York buildings were iconic: the Flatiron (1902), Metropolitan Life (1909), Woolworth (1913), Chrysler (1930), and Empire State Buildings (1931). After World War II, this same spirit prevailed as newer and equally iconic buildings arose: Lever House (1952), the Seagram Building (1958), the World Trade Center (1970), and the AT&T Building (1983).

For much of the last two hundred years, New York City's dense urbanism and its skyline of impressive buildings was a symbol of its power and wealth. There was a time, early on in the city's history, when the only man-made structures rising above the houses and trees were church steeples. The two-hundred-foot steeple of St. Paul's Chapel on Lower Broadway, built in 1764, was for a long while the tallest building in the city. That remained true until 1846, when Trinity Church rebuilt its steeple to a height of 284 feet and this became the city's tallest structure. Things did not change again until 1890 when George Post built the 309-foot high Pulitzer Building on Park Row. From that moment on, secular buildings reigned supreme. For many Americans, the steeple had been the symbolic transition between man on earth and the spiritual realm above. The challenge from commercial buildings changed the relationship between the god-fearing people of New York and their skyline. From the late nineteenth century onward, the commercial world overtook the religious realm and altered life in New York forever.

Early houses and commercial structures in New York were only five or six stories. By the 1860s, factory smokestacks poked up through the urban fabric but still not higher than the church steeple. Throughout the nineteenth century, the city grew and pressure to expand was enormous. Room to build in the traditional business districts was quickly exhausted and the only direction to go was upward. From the early nineteenth century onwards, the city's commercial structures grew from five floors to seven, then eight, nine, and by 1880, a ten-story building was normal. The chronicle of the fifty years between the ten-story buildings of the 1880s and the 102 stories of the Empire State Building in 1930 is the history of New York City and the United States.

The term "skyscraper" to designate the city's new, tall structures had a watery beginning. It was a nautical term for a specific sail on a tall-masted ship. In the 1870s, for example, the New York Times, recorded the colorful names of the sails on the Merry Dunn of Dover: "main mast, beginning at the lowest, viz. – Mainsail, topsail, top-gallant-sail, royal, sky-scraper, moon-raker, cloud-disturber, star-sweeper, heaven-poker, and jolly-jumper!" During the nineteenth century, the term was also in use in different spheres—equestrian, sports, fashion—but always keeping the meaning of tall or high in the air. One could speak of "a skyscraper mare," for a very large horse or "a 'skyscraper' throw to first base" in baseball, or ladies' "towering hats and sky-scraping plumes." The crossover to architecture occurred in 1883, in the New York-based magazine, *American Architect and Architecture*: "This form of sky-scraper gives that peculiar refined, independent, self-contained, daring, bold, heaven-reaching, erratic, piratic, Quixotic, American thought ('young America with his lack of veneration'). ...I should raise thereon a gigantic 'sky-scraper,' contrary to all precedent in practice, and I should trust to American constructive and engineering skill to build it strong enough for any gale." From that point onward, "sky-scraper" [hyphenated at first] became the universal term for a tall building.

Buildings have meaning. Anyone looking at the U.S. Capitol or the Kremlin in Moscow cannot help but think instantly of the powerful countries and political personages that these buildings represent. Anyone seeing the Eiffel Tower or the Great Wall of China is reminded of the technical prowess of the societies that built these great works. The Paris and Sydney Opera Houses invoke beauty and the cultural aesthetic of their eras. This vision of buildings is long-standing. A curious reader

in eighteenth-century Austria or France, upon seeing Johann Bernhard Fischer von Erlach's engravings of the Pyramids or the Nanjing Pagoda, would have been equally impressed by man's accomplishments. The same is true of New York's skyscrapers. From one building to the next, each represented what was most modern and commercially successful. The very essence of America changed, as they grew taller and taller.

In 1903, visitors to New York City bought penny postcards of the Flatiron Building to prove to their friends and families back home that such a wonder really existed. As the buildings grew taller and taller over the course of the twentieth century, although the price of the stamp increased from a penny, tourists to Manhattan still visited the island's tallest buildings and sent postcards home to friends and family to show how modern and successful New York was.

Birds-eye view of Trinity Church, c. 1846, then the highest man-made structure in the city. Schermerhorn Row in South Seaport, erected between 1811-12, the oldest extant commercial buildings in the city.

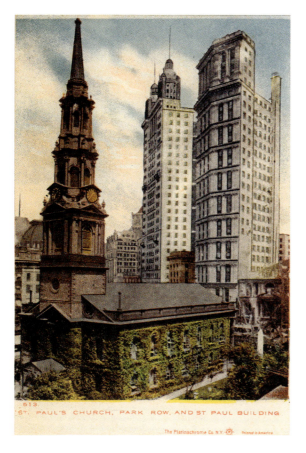 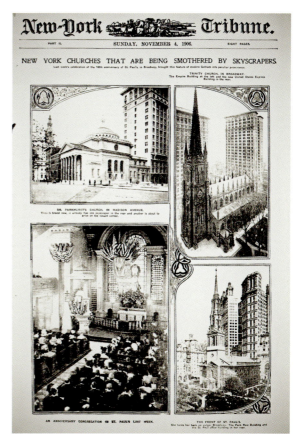

Through these postcards, even a farmer in Iowa or a cobbler in East Sussex could vicariously experience the wonders of the modern world.

London, Paris, and Vienna were prosperous cities because they were both the political and financial centers of their countries. Technically, New York City had been the political center of the newly founded American republic, but only for a few short period—between 1785 and 1790. It lost that status very quickly to Philadelphia for ten years before the American capital moved permanently to Washington, D.C., in 1800. At the dawn of the nineteenth century, New York was only a minor port compared to Philadelphia and Boston. It was not until 1825 when the Erie Canal opened a transit route between the Atlantic and the Great Lakes, that the port of New York flourished. It took only one generation after the canal opened for New York City to become America's greatest and most prosperous port. The quantity of goods moving through the city surpassed Boston, Baltimore, and New Orleans combined. By 1840, New York City had become the commercial hub of the United States.

As the docks grew to accommodate all the commercial traffic, so too did the urban fabric of New York City. The progression northward from city's traditional center at the Battery was constant as the city expanded to Park Place, then Madison Square, and onto Midtown, the Upper East and West Sides, and finally Harlem. In 1898, New York City's boundaries were expanded to incorporate Richmond County (Staten Island), Kings County (Brooklyn), Queens County (Queens), and land east of the Bronx River enlarging The Bronx significantly, creating a megalopolis of 360 square miles with 3,350,00 inhabitants. Manhattan was the center of this new conglomeration but was jammed with four and five-story buildings. As business boomed and the pressure to expand continued, there was nowhere to grow but upwards.

Late nineteenth-century technical innovation, combined with entrepreneurial spirit, aided the builders

Postcard of Trinity Church, 1880s, showing the church dwarfed by skyscrapers. *New York Tribune*, November 4, 1906, discussing how the churches are being swallowed up by the city.

Manhattan's Crowning Glories | 13

of tall buildings in this upward surge. No structure could rise high unless the engineers had access to strong, fireproof construction materials. The traditional building materials remained wood, stone, and brick just as building methods remained essentially the same. Ever since the Egyptians, beam and column construction continued to be an essential mode. Likewise, the arch—in use since the Greek and Roman ages—was the other traditional builder's tool. Whether using beam and column or arches, the weight of the walls supported the roof and the entire building. This approach was fine for small structures but not for large ones. The nine-story Great Apartment House from 1780 on Rue Valois in Paris is an example of an early tall building built this way. However, the problem in attempting high buildings prior to the nineteenth century was that the walls in the lower floors had to be extremely thick, resulting in rooms that were very small and had poor air circulation.

With the introduction of iron in the early nineteenth century and with the advancement of the mass production of steel by Harry Bessemer in the 1850s, engineers had new materials with which to work. Cast iron was an excellent material and had the strength of 50,000 lbs. per square inch, but steel's strength at 65,000 lbs. per square inch greatly surpassed that of iron. The single biggest disadvantage of iron came down to a small two-inch piece of metal; the nuts and bolts used to join beams were far inferior to the rivets used on steel support. Rivets were stronger than bolts, and steel quickly become the standard for all tall construction.

Engineers were then able to create an internal cage of structural steel that held up the floors, the walls, and the roof, all independent of the exterior wall. By the 1880s, for the first time in the history of man-made constructions, walls were not load-bearing. Rather than being the primary structural force, walls became a secondary element. Exterior walls were generally built after the steel core was erected, and were only needed to keep out the heat, cold, rain, and snow.

Johann Bernhard Fischer von Erlach, *The Pyramids,* from *Entwurff Eine Historischen Architektur,* 1721.

View of the City of New York, 1856. Souvenir folder, c. 1913.

Manhattan's Crowning Glories

They could be extensively pierced by windows to permit more light within, and ultimately, as we shall see, the entire exterior wall could be just glass. The introduction of steel created a true building revolution, and steel-cage construction with non-load-bearing walls became *de rigeur* for tall structures.

Fire was feared by all builders and all the more so with tall buildings. The Great Chicago Fire of 1871 proved that tall buildings could not rise until adequate fireproofing was available. Fire experts made buildings immeasurably safer by encasing the structural elements in brick or terra cotta. Marble replaced wood in hallways and public spaces, making the buildings much more fire resistant. It was impossible to make a truly fireproof building but technology and ordinance codes made sure that any fire would be slowed down so the inhabitants could escape.

The creature comforts of workers had to be assured before a tall building could be occupied. A primary concern was to give proper light and air to the workers, as well as ensure that adequate plumbing was available. With the placement of water tanks on all New York buildings over six floors, by the 1890s tenants could be assured of having running water on each floor for flush toilets as well as other personal uses. The invention of the incandescent electric light bulb in the 1880s by Thomas Edison allowed workers an additional source of light, especially needed as interior spaces became further removed from the windows.

The single most important technological advancement was an invention in the 1850s by a Vermont mechanic, Elisha Otis. His safety elevator was both a creative as well as an elegantly simple construction. A rope was attached to a wagon spring that was mounted to the top of the cab and connected to prongs on the side of the elevator. The prongs

Great Apartment House of 1780, 46, rue de Valois, Paris.   Stonehenge, an example of post and lintel architecture.   Spanish Romanesque Church, an example of an arched space.

ran along guide rails in an elevator shaft with teeth sticking out from it. If the rope were to break, the spring released and forced the prongs into the teeth along the shaft, thereby preventing the elevator from falling. Otis's invention was ingenuous and foolproof. During the 1853-54 Crystal Palace Exposition in the space that is now Bryant Park in Midtown Manhattan, Otis demonstrated his device to convince the public it was safe. In a dramatic display, he went up in an open lift and had the rope holding the platform aloft cut. The elevator did not fall, and public opinion was swayed.

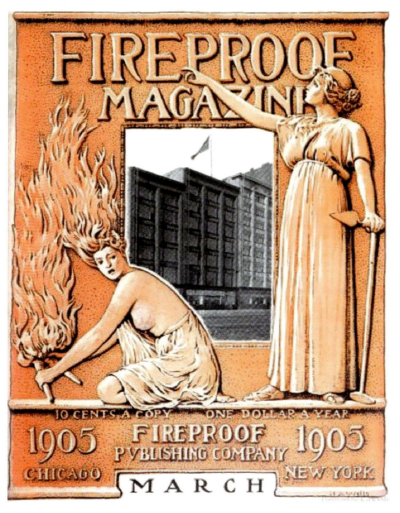

From these early beginnings, great technological innovations allowed the buildings to rise higher and more safely. Although steel cage construction has been the industry standard for almost a century, new technologies in bracing against wind have allowed buildings to rise to over one hundred stories. The slowing down of fire in buildings has improved significantly from cladding the beams in terra cotta. Asbestos was the mainstay of fireproofing buildings until the 1980s when regulations outlawed its use. Sprinkler systems have been used in commercial buildings since the mid-nineteenth century, although not mandated in skyscrapers until relatively recently. Indeed, the Twin Towers were retrofitted with sprinklers only in 2001, shortly before their destruction. Lighting technology advanced greatly since Edison's incandescent light. Florescent bulbs in the 1930s and walls of light in the post-war years allowed not only steadier light but also the ability to create dramatic lighting effects with the post-war glass boxes. Some have argued that

Superstructure of the Flatiron Building under construction, c. 1902.   *Fireproof Magazine*, dedicated to advancing techniques in fire prevention, 1905.

the key technological advance for skyscrapers has been the advent of central air conditioning. From the 1932 Philadelphia Savings Fund Society Building, the first air-conditioned structure in the United States, ventilation technology has created freestanding mini-climates in large buildings making them comfortable year round. Finally, the elevator has gone through many permutations. From the Otis hydraulic and cable elevators in the Eiffel Tower in 1889 to the world's fastest elevators traveling at 3,540 feet per minute in the 164-story Burj Khalifa in Dubai, improvements in elevator technology have allowed buildings to grow dramatically.

Although technology has allowed and abetted the rise of skyscrapers, entrepreneurs and industry visionaries were the driving forces for the erection of the buildings. Business magnates such as George Fulton, Frank Woolworth, Walter Chrysler, John J. Raskob, and Pierre S. du Pont recognized the advertising advantages of associating their companies with the power of enormously tall buildings. Corporations such at Metropolitan Life, Lever Brothers, Seagram, Pan Am, AT&T, and the New York Times understood how corporate identity is enhanced by erecting world-class buildings. As the financial capital of the United States, Manhattan has the highest concentration of significant skyscrapers. There is a symbiotic relationship between money, business, and great architecture.

Seen from afar, Manhattan's skyscrapers appear clustered into two major areas—lower Manhattan, focused around Wall Street,

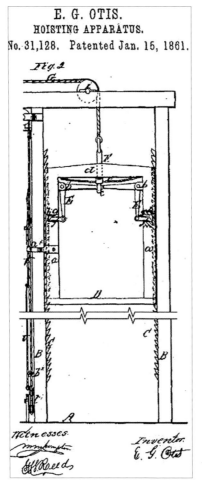

and Midtown Manhattan, centering around 42nd Street. For maximum stability, skyscrapers need to be anchored to bedrock and it was always said that these two business districts developed because the bedrock was closest to the surface in these two neighborhoods, thus reducing construction costs. Although a nice story, scholars have recently pointed out that this is a fallacy. Manhattan's skyscrapers were developed in these two areas because this was where manufacturing was historically located. This factor prompted zoning laws that encouraged large buildings in just those business districts and discouraged them elsewhere. Moreover, public transportation responded to these patterns by creating hubs in these areas, thereby further reinforcing these two main Manhattan business districts as the epicenters for New York's skyscrapers.

Skyscrapers were also shaped by the city's zoning laws. At first there were no real restraints and the driving force was to create buildings as tall and massive as possible to maximize rental space and profits. By the early twentieth century, skyscrapers were rising over the city in great numbers and the streets that surrounded them were becoming dark, foreboding canyons. The erection of the massive Equitable Building in 1916, at the time the largest office building in the world, was the straw that broke the camel's back. Because it was so high and built out as far as possible to the sidewalk, no daylight entered the surrounding streets. This behemoth sparked a public outcry that assured the authorities would enact new zoning laws to make the city more

Elisha Otis demonstrating the safety of his new invention at the Crystal Palace exhibition, New York, 1853. U.S. Patent granted to Otis for his safety elevator. .

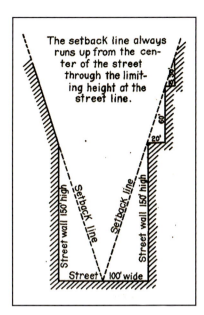

habitable. The 1916 Zoning Law not only regulated the heights of buildings but required setbacks at regular intervals, thus establishing a system that allowed sunlight to reach the city streets. This gave rise to the iconic wedding-cake look of the New York skyscrapers.

For 45 years, these zoning laws governed the work of architects and the appearance of Manhattan. It was not until 1961 that new zoning regulations were adopted. Le Corbusier's vision of an urban environment with commercial towers surrounded by open space had taken hold in America. The new 1961 Zoning Law continued the principle of set backs but also allowed buildings to rise straight up, monolithically, as long as there were airy, open plazas. The buildings on Sixth Avenue from 42nd Street to 57th Street prove the success of this new urban planning. Today a variety of zoning resolutions guide the hand of the architect. The overriding theme is that the public should have open spaces—indoors or outdoors—available to them. The 1977 Stubbins Associates Citicorp Tower and 1984 Philip Johnson AT&T Building are good examples of skyscrapers with open public spaces.

Manhattan's architecture also responded to the ever-changing demands of style. In essence, the evolution of the city's skyscrapers is a history of twentieth-century design. It has gone from neo-Gothic to Post-Modern and ecologically green over the course of the last 130 years. In the earliest years, the architects had no precedents for what a high-rise building should look like. Architects like Napoleon Le Brun, Cass Gilbert, and Daniel Burnham responded to an aesthetic that came from their training at the École des Beaux-Arts in Paris. Wanting to ensure that their buildings would stand the test of time, they designed them to look like famous European buildings but on a vastly enlarged scale. From French Renaissance to English perpendicular style, skyscrapers took on the appearance of palaces and cathedrals. After World War I, a younger generation of architects, such as William van Alen, Raymond Hood, William Lamb, Raymond Shreve, and Arthur Harmon abandoned traditional decorative vocabulary for the Art Deco style, or what was also called Moderne. Post World War II architects such as Mies Van der Rohe, Gordon Bunshaft, and Philip Johnson responded to the demands of Bauhaus modernism and the International Style. By the end of the twentieth century, architects such as Norman Foster, Frank Gehry, Renzo Piano, and the architectural firm FXFOWLE were responding to environmental and financial pressures to make their skyscrapers green and friendly to nature, and their architectural styles were literally outside the box. Breaking away from the glass box that had become the standard form of skyscrapers in the second half of the twentieth century, they sought daring new forms.

A diagram from the 1916 Commission on Building and Restrictions, establishing the rule for setbacks for all future buildings. A view showing the density of skyscrapers in Midtown and Lower Manhattan.

NEW YORK IN A FEW YEARS FROM NOW.
View from the Bay.

Thomas Nash's vision of New York City in the future, 1881.

As the height of buildings grew dramatically, politicians, writers, and planners all wanted to predict what the future of New York City would hold. Would it be a blessing or a nightmare? In 1881, a Thomas Nast cartoon in *Harper's Weekly* foresaw a city jammed with extravagantly tall buildings, each abutting the other, with only a single cavernous street running down the middle. The tiny spire of Trinity Church is in total shadow, trying to peak through the urban landscape. Twenty years later, at the turn of the century on December 30, 1900, a special supplement to Joseph Pulitzer's *New York World* ran an illustration of what the city would look like in 1999. It is an aerial view of Manhattan with enormous, twin-towered buildings topped with bulbous crowns. The buildings are so massive that they engulf the city, swallowing up the streets, and movement through the city is via sky-bridges and aerial taxis. A postcard issued in 1906 shows a similar view of the city looking up Broadway, with towering skyscrapers dwarfing the street and, as in the earlier vision of a future New York, the city is linked by sky-bridges and rapid transit is on aerial tracks that run through the buildings. Fantastic airships dot the skyline, perhaps a result of the Wright Brothers having circled the Statue of Liberty in a plane just a few years earlier.

These views of New York City over a thirty-year period are both prophetic as well as fanciful. The common thread among them is that lower Manhattan would be the center of the city's commerce and the city would be comprised of massive buildings rising up at times over 100 stories. They share a common belief that the urban fabric of New York would be incredibly dense—so dense that no land can be seen below, streets disappear, people are forced to move about along sky-bridges, and anything that is old (such as Trinity Church) is swallowed up by the new city. Some of these fears became reality, and for many today the city is a highly impersonal and overwhelming experience. But there was an overwhelmingly positive side as well. New York has remained a vibrant city where nothing remains static, and where the most advanced technology is always on display. Manhattan's buildings have become the soul of the city, its distinctive life force. Its skyscrapers are its crowning glory.

A postcard, *New York in the Future*, 1906.

Manhattan's Crowning Glories | 21

THE OLD NEW YORK TIMES BUILDING
ARCHITECT: GEORGE B. POST, COMPLETED 1889
1 PARK ROW (AT SPRUCE STREET)

Any discussion of a modern, technologically advanced New York Times Building will probably invoke an image of either the corporation's century-old building in Times Square or the new modern tower by Renzo Piano on Eighth Avenue and 41st Street. However, opposite City Hall in lower Manhattan, an earlier New York Times Building (presently Pace University) still stands in the heart of what was the nineteenth-century press district, known as Newspaper Row. In 1851, the *New-York Daily Times* was established in a nondescript converted house at 151 Nassau Street. It quickly outgrew its humble space and, in 1857, the fledgling newspaper commissioned a grand cast iron building on the corner of Park Row and Spruce Street. The architect, Thomas Jackson, built a state-of-the art five-story fireproof building with printing presses in the basement and typesetters on the upper floors. Thirty years later, in the late 1880s, Newspaper Row was booming with the offices of *The Tribune*, *The World*, *The Herald*, the *New Yorker Staats-Zeitung*, *The Evening Post*, *Sun*, and *The Journal*. As the newly built Potter Building towered over the five-story Times Building, George Jones, one of the founders of the paper, and the other owners of the *The New York Times* decided to erect an impressive building that would surpass that edifice and those of the other newspaper rivals. Rather than moving to a new location, the decision was taken to incorporate the older, still solid building into the new "modern" structure. The premier architect of the era, George B. Post, was engaged to create the Times' new home.

Post was a New York-based architect who had studied civil engineering at New York University and then apprenticed in the architectural studio of Richard Morris Hunt, one of the great nineteenth-century American architects. Hunt, who was the first American architect to study in Paris at the École des Beaux-Arts' prestigious school of architecture,

A view of Newspaper Row, c. 1900.

imbued upon his student a love of the classical Parisian tradition of design. Post specialized in commercial buildings and was the pioneer of tall buildings. In 1870, he designed the Equitable Building, the first commercial building to have an elevator. Other early accomplishments included one of the first skyscrapers, the ten-story Western Union Building (1875), and the interior metal-frame he conceived for the New York Produce Exchange (1884) closely approached the internal steel-cage construction that later became the standard for New York City's skyscrapers.

The sixteen-story 41 Park Row was planned as a Romanesque revival building. This Richardsonian Romanesque style, named after Henry Hobson Richardson, one of this country's earliest native born architects of world stature, favors heavy stone structures with soaring arches. It proved perfect for sturdy commercial buildings. While some preferred more Renaissance oriented architectural vocabulary, as is evidenced in the nearby Pulitzer building with its great cupola and dome, Romanesque was often used to suggest the sturdy masculine world of business. Respecting the wishes of the Times, Post merged the older Jackson building into the fabric of his new structure. He incorporated the most advanced technology into the project—especially the extra strong foundation that allowed the walls to be much lighter than those in similar buildings. The interior framing was exclusively

Thomas Jackson's original New York Times Building at 41 Park Row, 1888.

of iron and replaced the interior masonry walls of the original building

The façade consists of arches that diminish in scale as the building rises and shows Post's indebtedness to Richardson's architecture. Although the façades on the two streets are essentially the same, the Park Row side is longer and has an additional bay to the left. Despite this and other irregularities, there is a wonderful sense of balance and rhythmic harmony throughout the building. To top off his building, Post put a great Mansard-like roof with Gothic gables for windows. When Adolph S. Ochs arrived in 1904 to revive the failing newspaper, he had the Mansard-like roof removed and he ordered four additional floors, with a façade that skillfully harmonized with Post's original building. This is how it stands today.

George Post, the Old New York Times Building at 41 Park Row, c. 1900, before its upper stories were modified.

BAYARD-CONDICT BUILDING
Architect: Louis Sullivan with Lyndon P. Smith, completed 1898
65-69 Bleecker Street (between Broadway and Lafayette Street)

At thirteen stories, this building hardly qualifies as a skyscraper. But it was Louis Sullivan who made architects think about the nature of tall buildings. One of Sullivan's students, the great early twentieth-century American architect, Frank Lloyd Wright, told how Sullivan invented the form of the modern skyscraper after walking through downtown Chicago. Sullivan, according to Wright, came back to the office and made a sketch for the Wainwright Building in Saint Louis, declaring that skyscrapers were a new entity demanding a new, vertical aesthetic. He argued that pre-elevator buildings were low to the ground, squat, and horizontal. Now that technology allowed architects to build high, these proud, lofty towers needed new, vertically inspired designs.

In 1897, the United Loan and Investment Company bought a plot of land on Bleecker Street from the Bank for Savings to build a thirteen-story commercial building they intended to call the Bayard Building. As the building was coming to completion, the Bank for Savings recalled the mortgage and the property was taken over by Emmeline and Silas Condict. When the building was completed, the name was appropriately changed to the Condict Building in honor of the new owners. Yet within six months of the opening of the building, they sold it. Nonetheless, it has traditionally been referred to as the Bayard-Condict Building.

This is Sullivan's only skyscraper in New York City, and it expresses perfectly the principles he set forth in his essay, "The Tall Building Artistically Considered." He argued that the tall building must be "tall, every inch of it tall. It must be every inch proud to be a soaring thing...." The building has thick structural piers that run the height of the structure. These piers alternate with decorative, non-load-bearing colonettes that rise to the top of it. Visually, there is a graceful alternation of thick and thin. Sullivan's ornamentation under the windows is recessed so as not to take away from the verticality of the design.

One of the earliest terra cotta façades in New York, the walls of Sullivan's building are strikingly thin, especially when compared to the heavy masonry seen in most New York buildings. The terra cotta allows complex surface ornamentation in Sullivan's distinctive style. Although partly Romanesque and partly Moorish, it is nonetheless idiosyncratic and wonderfully ornamental. At the top, great winged angels arise out of the vertical piers. Their outstretched wings establish a horizontality that visually supports the cornice that crowns the building.

The Bayard-Condict Building did not directly influence the design of New York City's skyscrapers, but Sullivan's principles of expressing the verticality of the new, tall buildings influenced a generation of Beaux-Arts-inspired architects who confronted this challenge.

A detail of an angel under the cornice of the Bayard-Condict Building.

FLATIRON BUILDING
ARCHITECT: FREDERICK DINKELBERG FOR DANIEL H. BURNHAM & COMPANY, COMPLETED 1903
175 FIFTH AVENUE (AT 23RD STREET)

The popular Flatiron Building, originally called the Fuller Building, sits on a triangular plot of land at the intersection of Fifth Avenue and Broadway, two of New York's most important avenues. It is at the northern boundary of "Ladies Mile," the city's best shopping area at the turn of the century. The space is awkwardly narrow and pointed, creating challenges for any architect. The result was a remarkably tall, thin building that seized the public's imagination. Its elegantly tapered apex at 23rd Street looked to the public like the prow of a ship cutting through the fabric of the city.

Typical of early skyscrapers, the genesis of the building was fuelled by the strong personality of the patron as much as the architect who designed the structure. George Fuller created a very powerful, highly successful construction company in Chicago but he knew that New York was where success and fame lay. Accordingly, his company expanded to Manhattan, opening an office there in 1896. Fuller died suddenly in 1900 and his son-in-law, Harry Black, took over the reigns of the firm. The ambitious Black decided to build a skyscraper large enough to house the entire operation. In 1901, he turned to the famed Chicago architect, Daniel H. Burnham, who was known for designing and overseeing the World's Columbian Exposition in Chicago in 1893, as well as some early tall structures. At the time, there was no more successful architect than Burnham, whose firm was simultaneously undertaking work in Chicago, New York, Philadelphia, Boston, and Washington, D.C. As is often the case in a busy architectural firm, the Flatiron project was delegated to a younger colleague, in this case the forty-year old architect Frederick Dinkelberg.

Adhering to Burnham's Beaux-Arts vision, Dinkelberg designed and oversaw the construction of

The Flatiron Building under construction, 1902.

what would be come one of the world's earliest, iconic skyscrapers. His challenge was to balance Black's need for a rapid building schedule with Burnham's desire to slow down the process to ensure that the best material and workmanship was being used—a battle of wills that lasted the entire project. With buildings sprouting up all over New York, steel was at a premium. Using Black's connections in the construction industry, Dinkelberg was able to procure enough steel to allow the project to be completed in only fifteen months.

The design called for a triangular cage of steel covered with granite, brick, or terra cotta. Terra cotta, a product of fired, pressed clay, is used on the entire façade of the Flatiron Building except for the first four levels which are sheathed with granite. Terra cotta was a very popular building material at the time as it was cheap, strong, lightweight, and accommodated rich sculptural decoration. The Atlantic Terra Cotta Company in Tottenville, Staten Island, fabricated the thousands of pieces needed for the project.

There is a marked dichotomy between the rational, no-nonsense structural core of steel beams and the external sheath of highly decorative terra cotta. Dinkelberg cloaked the façade with French Renaissance ornament. At the street level, French rusticated columns were used—like those on the first level of the great

Parisian palace, the Louvre. At the fifth level, the terra cotta reliefs show alternating fleur-de-lis with heads of the goddess Medusa, the guardian against all evil. At the top of the building, looking onto Fifth Avenue, two putti hold aloft a shield adorned with the fleur-de-lis, but the meaning of the intended symbolism is lost. The Flatiron Building immediately captured the public's imagination. Both Alfred Stieglitz and Edward Steichen, two of America's most accomplished photographers, immortalized the building from different angles in all weather conditions. Equally, painters brought out the romantic side of the building. Although never the world's tallest structure, the Flatiron Building became New York's number one tourist destination. Indeed, it was celebrated world wide for its distinctive look. Visitors marveled at its great height and slender proportions, and they invariably sent home postcards showing how extraordinarily daring and truly modern New York was.

A detail of the terra cotta frieze from the Flatiron Building. The Porte des Lions on the façade of the Louvre Museum, Paris, compared to the entrance to the Flatiron Building. Facing page: a postcard of the Flatiron Building, 1902.

METROPOLITAN LIFE TOWER
ARCHITECTS: PIERRE AND MICHEL LE BRUN FOR NAPOLEON LE BRUN & SONS, COMPLETED 1909
1 MADISON AVENUE (AT 23RD STREET)

The Metropolitan Life Tower became a familiar building to hundreds of millions of working class Americans because it was prominently displayed on all insurance policies issued by the company. The company had been the first to pioneer low-cost insurance to immigrants who previously could not afford it, and this calculated business plan propelled it into the top tier of the insurance industry. In 1904, to meet the needs of the expanding company, John R. Hegeman, Metropolitan Life's president, had the company's architectural firm, Napoleon Le Brun & Sons, revise their previous 1890 designs for a corporate headquarters. The goal was to not only make a distinctive building to house the company's large work force but also to erect the world's tallest structure. Hegeman understood the advertising power of having the largest building in the world as its corporate symbol. Moreover, the insurance industry had been hit by a series of corruption scandals in the late nineteenth and early twentieth centuries. Although Metropolitan Life Insurance was not involved in any wrongdoing, the industry as a whole was tainted. Hegeman counted on swaying the hearts and minds of the public toward his company, and wanted the building to represent his firm's strength and integrity

Napoleon Le Brun was an architect responsible for many important early churches in Philadelphia and had designed several commercial buildings for the Metropolitan Life Insurance Company. Yet the task of designing and constructing the new headquarters fell to his sons, Pierre and Michel, after their father's death in 1901.

Everyone recognized that the great tower they designed was a reflection of the early sixteenth-century campanile in St. Mark's Square in Venice. In fact, it was no secret that Hegeman was fascinated by Venice and that Renaissance monument, and this complimented the Le Brun brothers' strong belief that the success of skyscrapers depended on adapting appropriate models from the past. Even more germane and poignant, the beloved Venetian landmark made headlines around the world when it suddenly collapsed in the summer of 1902, just before the planning of the Metropolitan Life Tower. Thus Hegeman and his architects erected not only a massive headquarters but also recreated a universally adored landmark. It is not a slavish copy, but a creative adaptation. In fact, it was twice the size of the Venetian tower, better built with a system of steel girders, and meant to last forever. Massive amounts of steel were

The Campanile in St. Mark's Square, Venice.

needed to create the internal superstructure, and the steel beams were fireproofed using state-of-the art technology with concrete rather than traditional brick or terra cotta sheathing.

Along with its neighbor, the Flatiron Building across the park, the Metropolitan Life Tower was an important addition to the skyline of New York. Its fame as the tallest building in the world lasted only four years, until the Woolworth Building surpassed it, yet it still maintained a special presence. It was one of the first of the city's buildings to be lit theatrically at night, and there is a dramatic carillon of massive bells in the clock tower. It offered a veritable sound and light show that enchanted New York citizens.

The Metropolitan Life crown at night. A postcard showing Madison Square with the Metropolitan Life and Flatiron Buildings, c. 1910.

The Metropolitan Life Building under construction, 1909.

Woolworth Building
Architect: Cass Gilbert, completed 1913
233 Broadway (between Barclay Street and Park Place)

The Woolworth Building reigned as the tallest building in the world from 1913 to 1929, marking a milestone in skyscraper construction. The forces that led to building high—elevators, steel cage construction, fireproofing, advances in plumbing and interior lighting—all reached a dramatic culmination in this iconic building. In 1913, the Woolworth Building was not only the most advanced technologically but it was also symbolic of the modern spirit in New York City and the country. It exemplified the newly-arrived twentieth century.

Frank W. Woolworth created a great commercial empire of "Five and Ten Cent" stores. At the turn of the century he had only fifty-nine stores and these were restricted to six East Coast cities. But by 1910, when he was planning his new headquarters, his company was transacting business from the Atlantic Ocean to the Rockies as well as in England, and his formidable commercial empire boasted 611 stores.

Woolworth hired Cass Gilbert to design a building that would house the headquarters for this company as well as for another venture in which he had a share, the Irving National Bank (today the Irving Trust Company). The original plan was to create a plain, medium height building of approximately fifteen floors. While on a trip to Europe, Woolworth was asked repeatedly about the Singer Building, the world's tallest structure, just across the park from where he intended to build his own headquarters. It dawned on him that having the world's tallest building would be incredibly good advertising for his five and ten cent stores, and so Gilbert was instructed to build the new edifice not only taller than the Singer Building, but also fifty feet higher than the newly-erected Metropolitan Life Tower which had since taken over as the world's largest building.

Cass Gilbert, designer of some of the most significant buildings in New York such as the U.S. Customs House in lower Manhattan

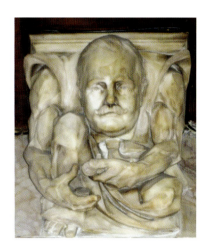

Corbel with Frank Woolworth paying for the building in nickels and dimes. The main entrance to the Woolworth Building.

and the twenty-three-story West Street Building, was considered the most important architect of his age. Although he had not studied at the École des Beaux-Arts in Paris, he was an advocate of the Beaux-Arts style. He believed that buildings should be beautiful, inspiring, and highly decorated. With their rich surface color and sculptural adornment, his buildings were a visual delight. Indeed, the Woolworth Building, with the exception of the limestone on the first four floors, was sheathed in terra cotta that was richly sculpted and occasionally colored.

Gilbert conceived the Woolworth Building as a thirty-story tower rising above a thirty-story base, the whole cloaked in the flamboyant Gothic style of the fifteenth century. It perfectly complemented the verticality of the building. Gilbert, like many of his generation, adapted great architecture of the past to fit modern purposes. Here he stressed allusions to the great medieval town halls of Europe and especially to Woolworth's favorite building, the Houses of Parliament in London. Gilbert wanted to "express the idea of a civic or commercial building rather than of an ecclesiastical one."

One enters the building through a Tudor arch whose many niches are fitted with small figures of laborers. Beyond is a superb lobby which, like the main nave of a church, is cruciform in shape and barrel vaulted. The ceiling is inlaid with highly colored glass mosaic tesserae, almost Byzantine in splendor. At the end of the nave, a dramatic flight of steps leads to the entrance of the Irving Bank. Bronze Gothic tracery adorns the marble walls as well as the elevator doors and mail chutes. At the ends of the transept are galleries with murals of Labor and Commerce painted by Carl Paul Jennewein. No space in the vast lobby was left undecorated—the medieval sensibility of horror vacui (fear of the void) reigns. Above the bank of elevators are small sculpted figures with amusing caricatures of people connected to the building, such as the architect Cass Gilbert presenting a model of the building, and Mr. Woolworth paying for it in nickels and dimes. The lobby's space is a tour de force of Gothic exuberance and twentieth-century capitalism. No wonder it was quickly dubbed, much to Gilbert's chagrin, a "Cathedral of Commerce."

Corbel of Cass Gilbert presenting the Woolworth Building. A view of the main lobby with the bank entrance at the top of the stairs. Facing page: the Woolworth Building compared to a great ocean liner, 1914.

Woolworth Building | 39

EQUITABLE BUILDING
ARCHITECT: ERNEST R. GRAHAM WITH PIERCE ANDERSON, COMPLETED 1915
120 BROADWAY (BETWEEN PINE AND CEDAR STREETS)

Never the tallest building in the world or even the most handsome, the Equitable Building became indirectly responsible for much of the distinctive character of the New York City skyline.

At the turn of the century, the Equitable Life Assurance Society was the world's largest insurance company in a very competitive but lucrative field. After its humble beginnings in 1859, the company made its mark in the years following the Civil War by innovating "incontestable life insurance" and creating what would be known as "group life insurance." Joining the cluster of banks and insurance companies in lower Manhattan, Equitable opened its grand headquarters in 1870. This structure was one of the first to use elevators, new fireproofing material, and an internal superstructure—not of steel but iron. In 1912, however, disaster struck when the building was devastated by a fire that destroyed the forty-year-old edifice.

Needing a new structure but not wanting to challenge the existing skyscrapers—the Metropolitan Life and Woolworth Buildings—that were captivating the public's imagination, the president of Equitable Life wanted only a commercially successful building. He went into partnership with Coleman Du Pont, of the Du Pont dynasty, to erect a substantial, modern office building. Du Pont engaged the architect Ernest Graham to design the largest one that could fit onto the lot. They wanted the most modern office building ever constructed. In particular, they wanted the most advanced elevator system in the world.

The final design was for a massive, H-shaped, thirty-eight-story block meant to hold over 16,000 workers. The largest office building in the world, it was to be like a self-sufficient ocean liner, only much larger. Stately and sober in aspect, the decoration was inspired by the Italian Renaissance. The exterior has traditional Corinthian pilasters, egg-and-dart molding, and massive arches. The lobby is adorned with a coffered ceiling.

The Equitable Building's fame is assured not because of its size or ornament but because it is considered the prime example of skyscrapers running amok and ruining the city. People in the neighborhood claimed that it

prevented fresh air from circulating, clogged the streets with masses of workers, and worst, cast a shadow six times its own area, stretching almost a fifth of a mile. Direct sunlight could not reach the surrounding streets. With both public and civic officials up in arms, a commission created new zoning laws to regulate the height of all future buildings in the city. Under the 1916 rule, all buildings had to be stepped back to allow sunlight to the street. This regulation created the iconic, wedding-cake look of New York's skyscrapers.

The old Equitable Building prior to a devastating fire in 1912. A postcard of the Equitable Building, c. 1916.

AMERICAN RADIATOR BUILDING
ARCHITECTS: RAYMOND HOOD AND J. ANDRÉ FOUILHOUX, COMPLETED 1924
40 WEST 40TH STREET (BETWEEN FIFTH AND SIXTH AVENUES)

The twenty-three-story black and gold tower, the American Radiator Building (presently the Bryant Park Hotel), designed by Raymond Hood and J. André Fouilhoux, was a revolutionary edifice. A *New York Times* review of the building in January 1924 concluded that Hood's building was unlike any other in the United States. Beautifully clad in black brick and trimmed with gold, the skyscraper, or so the reviewer believed, confronted the monotony and ugliness of older structures. Erected only twenty years after the Woolworth Building, it broke away from traditional Beaux-Arts ornamentation and led the way to a more modern tradition in designing skyscrapers.

The American Radiator Company was the premiere firm in the United States for providing steam and boiler heat to both commercial and residential spaces. It had made its fortune through the manufacture of steel boilers and cast iron radiators, and wanted a new building in Manhattan to serve both as its corporate headquarters as well as provide a world-class showroom for its products. The years after World War I were boom years for building great skyscrapers. The 1916 Zoning Law had altered the way architects conceived of tall buildings, and corporations increasingly embraced the idea of creating headquarters as a means of advertising their identity. Hood and his French-born partner, J. André Fouilhoux, received the commission to create a corporate headquarters for the American Radiator Company headquarters in the heart of Manhattan, on a prestigious site overlooking Bryant Park. This site allowed a splendid, unimpeded view of the tall building in all its majestic glory.

Raymond Hood had received classical training from the École des Beaux-Arts in Paris. In the early twentieth century, Hood worked for Cram, Goodhue and Ferguson, employing a standard neo-Gothic vocabulary. Hood's breakthrough

A postcard of the American Radiator Building, c. 1926.

came in 1922 when he joined forces with John Mead Howells and triumphed over 260 competitors to win the $100,000 prize to design what was supposed to be "the most beautiful and distinctive office building in the world," the Chicago Tribune Tower. Hood's winning design was still rooted in the traditional neo-Gothic spirit of the Woolworth Building, but with the American Radiator Building, Hood brought forth a more modern vision of skyscraper design. The American Radiator Building is conceived like a giant Gothic crossing tower. It may be only twenty-three stories high but the powerful surging rhythms of the massed elements create the illusion of a taller, powerful structure. The face rises straight up for fifteen stories like any office building, and then the setbacks begin, diminishing in scale as they rise to the dramatic crown of the building. The slightly curved corners of the tower emphasize the columnar, vertical essence of the elevation. The crown is conceived as a series of golden buttresses and arches, creating a broken, irregular silhouette much like that on a Gothic cathedral. But it is not the fussy type of archaeologically correct Gothic Revival style used previously. Rather, the many spires are bold, Cubist abstractions of expressive force. Moreover, especially around the entrance, one sees a mixture of other stylistic elements. Especially noteworthy are the stylized nude figures adorning the brackets around the doorway and on the third floor frieze.

The building stands out in New York City because of its striking color. Its use of black and gold is a daring experiment in color. The first two floors are faced with highly polished black granite, whereas the tower is done in black brick. Contrasting with this are the gold accents on the tops of the setback pinnacles as well as on the third story frieze. Originally the window coverings were golden as well. The arched pinnacle of the crowning tower adds the final touch of gold. The contrasts of color make the building stand out on the block, and provide a distinctive look. At night, the dramatic lighting makes it look like a giant glowing coal, appropriately symbolic for a radiator company.

After the great success of the American Radiator Building, Hood went on to design the Daily News Building, the McGraw-Hill Building, and several of the most prominent buildings in Rockefeller Center. Sadly, he died at the age of 53 from a heart attack, bringing an abrupt end to a wonderfully promising career.

A corbel above the entrance to the American Radiator Building. Facing page: the crown of the American Radiator Building.

American Radiator Building

Chrysler Building
Architect: William van Alen, completed 1930
405 Lexington Avenue (at 42nd Street)

No New York City building better represents the Art Deco style of architecture or the essence of skyscraper design than the Chrysler Building. When it opened in 1930, not only was it the world's tallest building but also it forever changed the nature of the city skyline.

As often is the case, the building started off as another project. The site was owned by the Cooper Union for the Advancement of Science and Art, and the original plans were for William van Alen to design a skyscraper for a former New York state senator, William Reynolds. The sixty-seven-story building was to be topped by a glass dome which would have shone brightly at night, as the jewel of the city's skyline. In 1928, Walter Chrysler, the Detroit car magnate, leased the site and the plans for the Reynolds project became the starting point for his building.

Chrysler, like many industrial leaders, had worked his way up from a job as a simple mechanic to a position where he oversaw one of the country's most important car companies, second only to Ford. By 1928, Chrysler was expanding his firm greatly and wanted a foothold in New York. He knew the symbolism of great architecture and he personally worked with van Alen to create a strong design.

William van Alen was a native New Yorker, born and raised in Brooklyn. He had a classical education in architecture, including a stay in Paris at the École des Beaux-Arts. He was concerned about turning away from European-inspired traditions and to apply principles of modern design to the skyscraper. Chrysler had van Alen alter the Cooper Union project to one that was more contemporary.

Art Deco became fashionable in the late 1920s. The influential 1925 Parisian fair, the Exposition Internationale des Arts Décoratifs et Industriels Modernes, had at its heart the promotion of French arts and design. At the same time, it exposed a generation of young architects, such as van Alen, to the possibility of replacing tired historical styles with romantic designs of a new age. Artists and designers embraced geometric patterns, bold, color, and industrial materials. For van Alen, this modern way of seeing the world epitomized the spirit that Chrysler wanted to express in his building.

The Chrysler Building is seventy-seven stories high and has setbacks which conform to the 1916 Zoning Law of New York. The first floor is clad in sleek black granite which contrasts with the white marble above. The entrance to the building is through a dramatic, polygonal arch of granite. The door is set into a frame of industrial glass and a special rustproof steel—emphasizing the use of modern materials. It is dramatically high and the angular design is unforgettable.

The frieze above the thirty-first floor with stylized racing cars.

The crown of the Chrysler Building.

The surface of the building above the fourth floor is white and gray brick with wonderful ornamentation appropriate to Chrysler and his company. The setbacks are bordered with chevron designs worked in brick, but still more dramatic is the frieze with stylized racing cars and polished steel hubcaps. At the corners of the setbacks are huge fifteen-foot gleaming steel Chrysler radiator caps. At the very top are large shining steel gargoyles in the shape of Chrysler hood ornaments. These symbols pay homage to the Chrysler Corporation and are conceived in the new Art Deco idiom.

The *pièce de résistance* of the building is the highly polished steel crowning spire with stylized sunbursts surrounding the triangular windows. At night the sunbursts are dramatically lit with fluorescent tubes, and this distinctive geometric pattern is thus visible from distant points around the city.

The building is a symbol of American technological progress. The walls were specially soundproofed, the wiring system was unique and easily adaptable, the elevators were the fastest that building laws allowed, the interchange between the subway and the building was direct, and the topmost floors under the steel crown were a very exclusive club, the Cloud Club.

The public interior spaces of the Chrysler Building are extravagant. Chrysler wanted people entering the ground floor lobby to not only be impressed but be "put in a frame of mind to work." The triangular lobby was constructed with rich, opulent materials. Most of the wall space was covered with a highly variegated and colorful red Moroccan marble. The floor, in contrast, is a yellowish travertine set in diagonal patterns to propel you into the building. Most remarkable are the lighting fixtures of Mexican onyx, designed in a stepped pattern to mimic the iconic stepped skyscraper outline.

The thirty-two elevators divided among four banks are works of art themselves. The outside of each elevator is a lotus pattern executed with a veneer of exquisite, imported woods. The interiors of the elevator cabs are each different, all abstract, geometric patterns inlaid in colorful, exotic woods.

The lobby's ceiling is covered with a large mural by Edward Trumbull. One of America's great muralists, Trumbull depicted "the vision, human energy and engineering ability which make possible the structure." The subjects are construction workers building the Chrysler Building, different forms of modern transportation, and a rendering of the exterior of the building. The warm colors of the mural complement the tones of the walls and floor.

The overall effect of the lobby and the elevators is visually stimulating, and fulfills Chrysler's wish that workers entering into such a beautiful space each day would be uplifted.

A detail of an airplane on the lobby ceiling by Edward Trumbull. The Lexington Avenue entrance to the Chrysler Building.

Chrysler Building | 49

Empire State Building
Architect: William Lamb for Shreve, Lamb, & Harmon, completed 1931
350 Fifth Avenue (at 34th Street)

A symbol of New York City for eighty years, the Empire State Building is the apex of the pre-war modern skyscraper. It is a 1250-foot high building with 102 stories, and the building held the title of tallest building in the world from its completion in 1931 until the north tower of the World Trade Center was erected in 1972. This midtown landmark is not only the most recognized building in the world but is a universal symbol of all tall buildings. The story of the Empire State Building is one of powerful rich men, national political intrigue, and a growing city.

It is hard to imagine that the plot of land on which the Empire State Building stands today was originally a farm, but when John Jacob Astor's father bought the land at Fifth Avenue and 34th Street in 1827, it was just pasture land. The Astors, the first multi-millionaires in America, made their considerable wealth from trading in fur and wise real estate investments. Just twenty years after the Astors bought the Fifth Avenue property, it was one of the choicest areas in growing Manhattan. In fact by 1859, the Astor brothers, John Jacob Jr. and William B., gave up their downtown residence at Astor Place to build new palatial homes on Fifth Avenue at 33rd and 34th Streets so as to be near the homes of the Vanderbilts and other "merchant princes" of New York. In the early years of the twentieth century, the character of the area changed yet again, and the sons and relatives of John Jacob Jr. knocked down their family homes to build two hotels – the Astoria and the Waldorf. These hotels were then joined to form the now famous New York institution, the Waldorf-Astoria Hotel. In 1929, the Astors sold the land under the forty-year-old hotels to a real estate speculator, John J. Raskob.

The life of John J. Raskob is an American tale of a Catholic child from a poor family who grew up to become an industrialist, a self-made millionaire, and a politically influential person. He worked as Pierre Du Pont's private secretary and ended up becoming the treasurer and vice-president of E.I. Du Pont de Nemours, the great chemical concern in Delaware. He advanced with Du Pont to General Motors, where he served as the treasurer and vice-president

A 1930s view of the Empire State Building with many unoccupied floors unlit.

To create a successful skyscraper like the Chrysler, Woolworth, or Metropolitan Life buildings, structures whose corporate ownership created their identities, Raskob decided to borrow the official nickname of New York State, the "Empire State," and to have as the building's spokesman one of the most popular New York and American politicians, Al Smith. The combination of the great size of the building with the celebrity status of Smith was a marriage made in heaven.

Raskob sought a no-nonsense practical architectural firm and turned to Shreve, Lamb & Harmon, which he knew well from his days at General Motors. They were known as commercial architects who embraced the new International Style. William Lamb, a New Yorker, was the principal designer on the project. He particularly liked simple, classically modern buildings. He considered the Chrysler Building too flamboyant and over-decorated, and conceived a very different building. Although there are Art Deco elements in the decoration, such as the spandrels under the windows, in general the ornament is far more sparse than at the Chrysler Building.

in charge of the company's finances and became a very wealthy man. He was a great supporter of the popular, four-time New York State governor, Al Smith (who was also Catholic). When Smith ran as the Democratic candidate for president of the United States in 1928, Raskob was appointed chair of the Democratic Committee even though he was a conservative Republican. Despite Smith's loss to Herbert Hoover (some blamed Raskob for shifting Smith's views too far to the right), Smith and Raskob remained great friends.

Raskob's vision for his new building was clearly defined: it was to be financially successful. To do this, he wanted to construct the tallest building in the world with the most rentable space. By the 1920s, skyscrapers were great forms of advertising and Raskob knew he needed a gimmick to succeed.

Raskob set very strict conditions for his architects—a fixed budget, no space more than twenty-eight feet from a window to corridor, an exterior of limestone as high as possible, and it had to be completed by May 1, 1931, a year and six months after the beginning of the project.

Lamb conceived of his building as a tall spire with a series of setbacks

The Fifth Avenue entrance to the Empire State Building.

starting at the fifth floor, which is lower than normal. Despite the building's dizzying height, the low, five-story base gave pedestrians in the street an almost intimate feeling. Because of the generous setbacks all around the building, a natural well of light surrounds the building, guaranteeing the tenants light and fresh air, one of Raskob's important requirements. A mast at the very top was originally intended for mooring dirigibles but the concept of such an airport soon proved impossible. Nonetheless, the mast adds the equivalent of fourteen floors in height, and there is a two level basement, thus setting the building at a grand total of 102 floors. Finally, in 1953 a great two-hundred-foot tower television antenna was added, giving the building its distinctive post-war look.

Raskob wanted the entrance to be as dramatic and grand as the building. Yet, compared to the great Art Deco lobbies of the time, the lobby of the Empire State Building is straightforward and rather uncomplicated. It embodies Lamb's vision for a grand entrance to the building—simple and elegant. Like a chapel, it is tall, narrow, and focuses on the end wall that contains a massive aluminum relief of the Empire State Building with a giant radiant sun behind it. Originally, there also was an anemometer that measured the wind speed where the dirigibles were supposed to dock above, but this was eventually replaced by a clock. Curiously the designations N, S, E, W remain in place of the numbers 12, 3, 6, 9. The terrazzo floor has a zigzag pattern in black propelling the visitor toward the great relief of the building. The celestial ceiling executed in gold, platinum, and aluminum leaf, and with a design of cogs, gears, circles, and stars, was recently restored to its original glory. With its use of rounded corners, love of a machine aesthetic, and limited ornamentation, the lobby represents the best of "Streamlined Moderne," a style popular in the United States in the 1930s.

An image from a 1936 issue of *Popular Science Magazine* showing a zeppelin mooring on the Empire State Building. The relief in the lobby showing the Empire State Building.

Rockefeller Center

Architects: Associated Architects made up of Corbett, Harrison & MacMurray; Hood, Godley & Fouilhoux; and Reinhard & Hofmeister, Phase 1 completed 1939; Phase 2 completed 1973

48th to 52nd Streets between Fifth and Sixth Avenues

The story of Rockefeller Center is a tale of powerful people, great wealth, and wonderful art. The complex has nineteen interconnected buildings on twenty-two acres. The original project was for fourteen buildings and was started in the 1930s; an additional seven buildings, begun in 1947, were completed by different teams of architects. The complex is very much part of the American spirit. It is the home of the Rockettes and the Rainbow Room, as well as the site of the famous annual Rockefeller Center Christmas tree; it is the home of one of America's first radio and television networks, the National Broadcasting Corporation; and is today the locus for an award-winning NBC television show: *30 Rock*.

The history of the development of Rockefeller Center is complex and starts more than a century before Mr. Rockefeller opened the first building. In 1801, this area was just open fields. A Columbia College physician, David Hosack, purchased the land for only $3000 to create the best American garden, especially for plants with medicinal properties. On what is now the Channel Gardens, he built a great greenhouse for his teaching botanical garden. By 1807, he had put so much of his own money into the gardens that he was bankrupted and was forced to sell it. Through his many political connections, he persuaded the state of New York to buy it for $7,500. Three years later, the gardens were totally overgrown and had gone to seed.

In 1810, Columbia College, strapped for money, turned to the State of New York for funding. The state, short of cash but wanting to help, gave the college this dilapidated plot of land instead. The Upper Estate, as it was renamed, was of no real use to the college and so it was rented out to farmers for a paltry sum. In 1811, the city fathers imposed a grid plan on Manhattan and the Upper Estate fell right into the center of what would one day become very valuable property.

Columbia never developed the Upper Estates. By the dawn of the twentieth century, the twenty-two acres was a ramshackle group of three- and four-story commercial

An engraving of the Elgin Garden Greenhouse, 1804.

Rockefeller Center | 55

buildings. The Roman Catholic cathedral of New York stood opposite the property, but the neighborhood was seedy, albeit profitable. The rent from the rooming houses, brothels, speakeasies, shoe repair shops, and jazz clubs brought the university about $300,000 in rent per year.

The last piece to the puzzle in the development of Rockefeller Center was the need to replace the aging Metropolitan Opera House. An opera house had been built in the early 1880s on Broadway at 39th Street with the help of some of New York's richest families—the Vanderbilts, the Morgans, and the Rockefellers. By the 1920s the opera house was antiquated and faded, with bad acoustics and worse sight lines to the stage. The owners decided to approach John D. Rockefeller, Jr., known to most as "Junior," to create a business complex on the plot of land owned by Columbia with a new opera house as its anchor.

The Rockefellers were among America's richest families. John D. Rockefeller, Senior, founder of Standard Oil, had an immense personal fortune. "Junior" was in charge of philanthropy, and his projects were impressive. He supported hospitals, created national parks, built colonial Williamsburg, and restored Versailles. Much to everyone's surprise, Junior approved the plan for the complex and opera house.

In January 1929, Junior signed a lease with Columbia to rent eleven acres of the Upper Estate for $3 million per year for twenty-four years, with an option to renew three times for twenty-one years each. If the Rockefellers took the full option, the lease would run through all of the twentieth century. If they chose not to renew at any point, the land and everything on it would revert to Columbia.

From this point on, it was only a question of finance. Junior's concern was not loosing money. There were long discussions about the nature of the complex. Some thought this could be a good transportation center, with trains bringing people in from New Jersey, and a double-decker roadway could make this area a hub for commuters. A major concern was whether the opera house would be financially sound and what would occur during the day when the theater would be dark and would draw no pedestrian traffic to the complex. Junior was quickly loosing interest in the opera house but was very enthusiastic about the commercial complex.

The *New York Times* ran a front-page story on Tuesday, October 29, 1929, "Architects Picked To

A view of the Channel Gardens and 30 Rockefeller Plaza. Maps of Columbia University's Upper Estate and the Rockefeller Center complex.

Plan Rockefeller Centre, Which May Have Opera House As A Nucleus." To oversee the project, Rockefeller hired a lawyer, John R. Todd, who was decidedly against the opera house. As fate would have it, sharing the news that day on the front page of the *New York Times* that day was, "Stock Prices Slump $14,000,000,000 In Nation-Wide Stampede To Unload…" It was Black Tuesday and the announcement of the Great Wall Street Crash of 1929. With the turmoil of the stock market crash, Todd and Rockefeller abandoned the opera house and focused exclusively on the idea of a commercial complex.

The project was massive and would be the largest building campaign in the city's history by a private individual. The immediate problem was taking control of the 203 lots with 228 buildings that held 5000 tenants and thousands of leases and subleases. After much drama, all the leases were acquired save two: the Maxwell property on the corner of Sixth Avenue and 50th Street and the Hurley-Daley property on the corner of Sixth Avenue and 49th Street. No matter what the agents of Rockefeller did, the two holdouts would not sell. In the end, Rockefeller gave up trying and altered the footprint of the entire complex and built around them. Today, the two hold out properties are still there.

Teams of architects worked on the project over the course of its construction. Rockefeller and his associates wanted a great architect for this project; the problem was that architects have strong personalities, and great architects have the strongest personalities.

Rockefeller wanted nothing to do with strong personalities. He wanted someone who would be cooperative. Raymond Hood, who had just built the popular American Radiator Building, became the lead architect of the new complex for a short time. Rockefeller preferred nineteenth-century French Beaux-Arts buildings but nonetheless encouraged Hood to design something in a modern style as he had just done in the Radiator Building.

Hood and his fellow architects created one of the first skyscrapers in New York that embraced the concept of a giant office slab. As the 1916 Zoning Law applied to the entire property including the lower national buildings fronting Fifth Avenue and the soaring RCA and International Buildings in the middle, the ratio of shorter buildings to the taller ones allowed them to dispense with setbacks. 30 Rockefeller Plaza could have risen as one thin seventy-story slab. However, Hood added setbacks to give the building sculptural richness. Nonetheless, the overall thinness of the building is significant and presages the form of the skyscraper in the post-war years. Hood died very young, at the age of 53, while he was in the midst of Rockefeller's project. Luckily, he had completed enough of the project to give it his imprimatur.

After a European tour one summer, Rockefeller had the brilliant idea of dedicating the four smaller buildings facing Fifth Avenue to various countries: France, England, Italy, and Germany. He hoped that people and businesses associated with those countries—consulates, national shipping lines, tourist offices—would rent space and work in those buildings. Indeed, the great shipping companies such as Cunard and the French and Italian lines had their offices here. This is where you came to buy your tickets and class distinctions were maintained. First class passengers were on the street level while tourist passengers had to go to the basement.

La Maison Française, the British Empire Building, the Palazzo

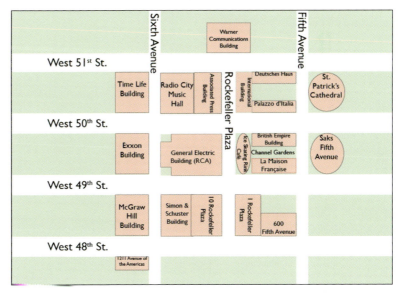

d'Italia, and Deutsches Haus were planned. In a stroke of genius, the space between the French and English buildings was named "the Channel Garden" after the body of water that separated France from England. However, the building dedicated to Germany quickly posed problems for Rockefeller and his team. The mid-1930s, when the buildings were going up, was not a good time to embrace Nazi Germany or things German. Plans to replace it with one dedicated to the Soviet Union were similarly abandoned. An International Building was conceived, dedicated to global peace.

The anchor of the International buildings complex was the U.S. Passport Office. While waiting for passports, travelers would encounter international banks and travel agencies, great international airlines and shipping lines, and tourist offices from all over the world. Your trip really started here.

The centerpiece of the International Building was Lee Lawrie's sculpture, *Atlas Supporting The World*. It was intended to represent this new internationalism and to counterbalance the entrance to St. Patrick's Cathedral across Fifth Avenue. The religious and secular worlds were set in apposition.

Rockefeller Center was to be alive with art—great murals and sculpture. A coherent scheme of decoration was to inspire visitors. Rockefeller called together a high-level committee with some of the country's leading museum curators, practicing artists, and other advisors. The leading voice was a philosopher from Scripps College, Hartley Burr Alexander. He chaired the committee and devised a series of five lofty themes to run throughout the complex: Man's progress towards civilization of today, Man's development in mind and spirit, Man's progress along physical and scientific lines, Man's progress in industry, and the Character of the nation.

The decoration on the façades of the national buildings was created largely by artists associated with those countries. The main panel over the door of La Maison Française is by Alfred Janniot, a great French sculptor, who created a relief of Friendship between France and America. The two women with intertwined arms are symbols of Paris and New York. Paris sits on a boat (her traditional symbol) and holds a model of Notre Dame, while New York sits on a more modern ship and is in front of the lower tip of Manhattan. Below are three figures representing Poetry Beauty, and Elegance—aspects of French culture and commerce. The demure figure of Beauty, combing her hair, is totally nude and proved quite controversial because in 1932 New York, a fully frontal nude woman on Fifth Avenue was considered shocking to some. Certainly Rockefeller was quite upset but to counter his objections, it was argued that most people would not really see it as they quickly walked by.

A view of the International Buildings on Fifth Avenue.

The decoration on the British Empire Building symbolizes the riches of Britain and its colonies. Unlike the other national buildings, the British Empire Building embraced non-British artists such as the German-American, Carl Paul Jennewein and the Italian-American, Attilio Piccirilli. The latter carved Great Britain's coat of arms. Jennewein sculpted a series of figures representing the industries of the British Empire. Appropriately, the stylized sun at the bottom represents the famous phrase: "The sun never sets on the British Empire."

The 1935 design by Attilio Piccirilli for the panel over the doorway to the Palazzo d'Italia showed a young man digging, surrounded by political inscriptions associated with Mussolini and Italy's fascist government. Similarly the four stone panels at the top of the façade by Leo Lentelli represented the great ages of Italy. The last relief was controversial because it showed bundled rods symbolizing unity, an eagle, and "AXII" for Anno XII (the twelfth year of the fascist regime). Piccirilli's relief was boarded over and replaced in 1963 with sculpture by Giacomo Manzù. The "AXII" was chiseled out after World War II, but the rest of the fascist imagery remains in place.

The Channel Garden slopes down toward the main plaza space, which serves as a café in the summer and an ice skating rink in the winter. The walk down the gentle slope is a conscious architectural devise to get the public into the heart of the complex. This central plaza was America's public square. Rockefeller wanted this area to have a community spirit. It was to

Alfred Janniot, *Friendship between America and France*, 1934, on La Maison Française. Attillio Piccirilli, *Art = Labor*, 1935, formerly on the Palazzo d'Italia. Carl Paul Jennewein, *Industries of the British Empire*, 1933, on the British Empire Building.

Rockefeller Center | 59

be a destination to which people would travel and spend time and money.

Rockefeller decided to build the complex in two phases. Phase one included the international buildings and the main seventy-story skyscraper just behind the main plaza. Rockefeller needed an important corporate anchor to his complex, and went to RCA, the Radio Corporation of America, which was advancing the new field of radio and television. David Sarnoff, the founder of RCA, was the person with whom Rockefeller and Todd worked. RCA took one third of 30 Rockefeller Plaza which not only gave an important central focus to Rockefeller Center but it also determined much of the iconographic program in this central area of the complex.

Rockefeller wanted a striking work of art at the main entrance to 30 Rockefeller Plaza, and his committee engaged Lee Lawrie, one of America's great modern sculptors, to undertake this. His great work is the complex imagery of *Wisdom—A Voice from the Clouds*, flanked by reliefs of *Sound* and *Light*, the chief disseminators of wisdom. Wisdom hovers over the main entrance. With one extended hand he holds a compass, and with the other he parts the clouds of ignorance. The huge compass is both drawing the cosmic forces as well as controlling them, and these forces spread down through the glass screen below. Above are the words: "Wisdom and knowledge shall be the stability of thy times." The image is borrowed from a work by the English romantic artist, William Blake. In Blake's work, God the Creator is depicted as an architect who controls and creates everything. Lawrie has transformed this imagery into a secular creator and controller whose new credo is technology—electricity, radio, and television.

The most famous sculpture in Rockefeller Center is Paul Manship's *Prometheus*. In the summer, playful water jets spurt upward behind the sculpture. Prometheus is a Titan, the son of the gods of Heaven and Earth, and brother to Atlas. A champion of humankind and known for his keen intelligence, he stole fire from Zeus and gave it to mortals. Prometheus is credited with—or blamed for—playing a pivotal role in the early history of mankind by bringing fire and civilization, but here that gift of divine fire, held aloft in his right hand, is the electricity which brings us radio and television—the new forces of civilization. It is a clever program of mankind's progress. Especially when seen at a distance and with Lawrie's reliefs in view, it constitutes an important homage to Rockefeller Center's major tenant.

William Blake, *The Ancient of Days*, 1794. Lee Lawrie, *Wisdom—A Voice from the Clouds*, 1940.

The lobby of 30 Rockefeller Plaza offered huge expanses of wall space for murals. Abby Rockefeller, Junior's wife, and the artistic committee engaged three great muralists to decorate this area: the Spaniard, Jose Maria Sert, the Englishman, Frank Brangwyn, and, the famous Mexican muralist, Diego Rivera. Rivera was an artist promoted by Abby and her son, the future governor of New York and Vice President of the United States, Nelson Rockefeller. The theme of the lobby was "New Frontiers," not only American frontiers but new global ones. Each muralist had his assignment. Brangwyn was to depict mankind's ethical development. Sert was to represent man's development of technological power. Rivera was to express "man at a crossroads looking with uncertainty but with hope and high vision toward a new and better future."

A great controversy arose over Rivera's mural. In April 1933, the artist and his wife, Frida Kahlo, came to New York and started work. His fresco was to cover the entire wall and even wrap around to the elevator banks on each side. Despite his anti-capitalist views, the Rockefellers adored him, at least at first. However, his *Man at the Crossroads* portrayed the ills of modern capitalist society too blatantly

Paul Manship, *Prometheus*, 1934 below 30 Rockefeller Plaza.

for his patrons. The massive mural depicted women drinking alcohol, cells representing sexually transmitted diseases, the revolutionaries Leon Trotsky and Vladimir Lenin—all of which upset Junior greatly. When the architects and Nelson Rockefeller found out, they approached Rivera and asked him to replace them. Rivera wrote back and said he would not but would add Abraham Lincoln. A satisfactory compromise could not be reached and so Rivera was paid the $21,000 remainder of his contract and was dismissed. Rivera was unaware that one clause stipulated that Rockefeller had the right to determine whether the work would be displayed. There was public outrage. The day he was paid off, the fresco was covered with brown paper. There was thought that it would be moved to the newly formed Museum of Modern Art, but it was too big to transport. Nine months later, on a Saturday night, workmen destroyed it.

The dilemma was what to do with this space. Rockefeller thought a big clock would be good but this was ultimately rejected. By 1936, Jose Maria Sert was asked to come up with a new plan. His project, titled American Progress, is a vast allegorical scene which balances opposites. Men erect various statues, some representing the muses of Poetry, Music, and Dance, others representing labor. Among the great men of the past depicted, Lincoln, the man of action, is counterbalanced by Ralph Waldo Emerson, the great thinker. In the background is a depiction of Rockefeller Center, a place where action and ideals meet.

Brangwyn's murals in the South Corridor are equally optimistic. The basic theme is "Man in search for truth and happiness must learn to accept the teachings of Christ." However, John Todd did not think that the introduction of Christ into a business setting was the best idea, but they were so behind schedule that they were obliged to let Brangwyn proceed. The four murals, installed in 1934, used the same muted palette as Sert's compositions. The first mural, The Sermon on the Mount, bears an inscription: "Man's ultimate destiny depends not on whether he can learn new lessons or make new discoveries and conquests, but his acceptance of the lesson taught him close upon two thousand years ago." The hooded figure in the upper part of the mural was the key problematic figure. It is supposed to be unclear but most people see it as Christ. Brangwyn's work expresses Rockefeller's desire to have a "high" moral tone in his complex.

The columns, the marble flooring, and stairway banisters were intended to evoke the atmosphere of an elegant ocean liner. In some ways, Rockefeller wanted to give

José Maria Sert, detail of American Progress, showing Lincoln and Emerson building a better world, 1937.

both visitors and workers a sense that they were on a voyage and would be transported from the everyday world to a special space. The topmost floor of 30 Rockefeller Plaza is an observation deck. The deck was originally designed to evoke the upper decks of a 1930s grand ocean liner, complete with deck chairs and large air conditioning vents and other funnels painted in bright colors.

Because the complex has buildings of varying heights, gardens were created on the roofs of the lower buildings. Rockefeller thought that workers looking out to these seven acres of gardens would be soothed and calmed. Of course, any office that offered such views paid higher rents.

Rockefeller Center was primarily a place of business. But it was also planned to be a place to play and be entertained. Replacing the opera house, which would have had only a limited though influential audience, was Radio City Music Hall. This space was intended to have entertainment that appealed to the masses. Even the use of "Music Hall," a lower class form of entertainment, was meant to be a term of endearment for many of the theatergoers. This was not an ordinary movie theater because it also featured live entertainment. It boasted major singers and comedians, a live orchestra, and perhaps most famous of all, the Radio City Rockettes. For Rockefeller, Radio City Music Hall became yet another avenue of revenue for the complex but, beyond that, it became a place for family-friendly fun and, ultimately, a symbol of New York City. The Rockefellers renewed their lease several times. In 1985, Columbia University sold the land of the complex to the Rockefeller Group for $400 million. A few years later, in 1989, the entire complex was sold to the Japanese corporation, Mitsubishi. The 1990s were financially difficult years and Rockefeller Center was one-fourth empty. Mitsubishi retained the Sixth Avenue side but sold off the oldest buildings to the current owners, Tishman Speyer, a management firm, for $1.85 billion. From the time Rockefeller inaugurated the complex in 1933 to the annual lighting of the Christmas tree, Rockefeller Center is the heart and soul of the vibrant city of New York.

José Maria Sert, detail of *American Progress*, showing the Muses, 1937.

LEVER HOUSE
ARCHITECT: GORDON BUNSHAFT FOR SKIDMORE, OWINGS & MERRILL, COMPLETED 1952
390 PARK AVENUE (BETWEEN 53RD AND 54TH STREETS)

Lever House, the headquarters of the Lever Brothers Company, is a small twenty-four-story office building clad in glass and stainless steel. It is composed of two unadorned slabs: a vertical tower resting on a horizontal base. As unassuming as the building is today, it was the first great post-war American skyscraper and influenced high-rise design for a generation of architects. As *Life Magazine* wrote in its June 2, 1952, issue: "Shiny New Sight, Soapmaker's Washable Building is World's Glassiest." Through its use of glass and steel, the rejection of all ornament, and lack of setbacks, the building started a new design tradition in New York and the United States.

At the time, the Lever Brothers Company was the American subsidiary of an English soap company founded by William Lever and his brothers in 1887. From one product, Sunlight soap, the Levers' corporate fortune expanded dramatically—at first with personal cleaning products such as Lux, Lifebuoy, and Vim, and later with laundry detergent such as Tide.

In 1929, Lever Brothers merged with a Dutch concern, Margarine Unie, to form the multi-national corporation, Unilever. By 1949, Unilever wanted to consolidate its North American headquarters in New York City. The company president, Jervis J. Babb, an architect who had studied under Frank Lloyd Wright and worked with him at the Johnson Wax Building in Racine, Wisconsin, understood the importance of corporate identity through architecture. Babb hired Skidmore, Owings & Merrill (SOM) to create a building that would represent modern architecture at its best. SOM brought the new European modernism, known as the International Style, to the United States.

A principal exponent of the International Style within the company was Gordon Bunshaft. He was born in Buffalo, attended the prestigious Massachusetts Institute of Technology, and from 1935 to 1937 toured Europe on special travel fellowships. While on his European tour, he saw firsthand the work of architects such as Walter Gropius, Le Corbusier, and Robert Mallet-Stevens. Bunshaft's design for Lever House embodies many of the principles that he witnessed abroad—embracing modern materials for an industrial aesthetic and rejecting ornamentation. His glass and steel building looks almost sterile—a perfect, squeaky-clean image for a soap company.

The monolithic slab skyscraper had precedence in New York. The thin, seventy-story building at 30 Rockefeller Plaza set the stage for this new look. Moreover, rising at the same time as Lever House was the United Nations Secretariat. The great French architect Le Corbusier conceived the basic elements of the original building, but the American architect, Wallace Harrison, worked out its details. The Secretariat was a tall, thirty-nine-story slab whose ends are faced with marble but its major expanses are glass. The Lever House and the Secretariat brought the glass curtain wall to New York City and established the model of what the new post-war skyscraper would be.

Lever House was a series of firsts. It was the first skyscraper to avail itself of the floor-area-ratio principle of New York urban zoning.

Le Corbusier, *Villa Savoye*, Poissy, France, 1931.

It did not need to have setbacks because it is built on only one fourth of the property. It was the first New York City skyscraper to not build to the property line and to create a ground floor garden open to the sky. It was the first building to start the rentable space on the second floor. It was the first building to transform the lobby from a commercial area to a large empty space with the elevators contained in just one corner It was the first building to totally embrace un-openable glass windows and a technically advanced ventilation and air-conditioning system. It was the first building to have siding supported by structural steel in the inside. These firsts did not come without challenges.

The critical reception of the building was immediate and positive. To the public, the building was remarkable because it did away with the customary solid masonry walls of the city. As people walked past, they paused and marveled at this new aesthetic. At the opening of Lever House, the mayor of New York predicted that this would be "The building of tomorrow which promises to set the pattern for the city of tomorrow." The architectural critic Lewis Mumford saw the building as "the first office building in which modern materials, modern construction, and modern functions have been combined with a modern plan." For the architectural professional, it was an expression of a new age. It showed architects how to break the "street wall," and how to employ a glass curtain wall in an elegant fashion.

With just twenty-two floors, Lever House is one of the smaller skyscrapers in Manhattan. Despite its size, it was the prime expression of the International Style in this country. There are those who claim this building was responsible for the style of the glass box that, in the hands of lesser architects of the late 1950s and '60s, destroyed all sense of style in architecture. The modernist adage, "Less is more," coined by Mies van der Rohe to describe the elegant minimalism of the International Style, devolved, some critic said to, "Less is less." Yet no one would ever accuse the Lever House of being ordinary, although many of its children and grandchildren were not as fortunate.

SEAGRAM BUILDING
ARCHITECT: LUDWIG MIES VAN DER ROHE WITH PHILIP JOHNSON, COMPLETED 1958
375 PARK AVENUE (BETWEEN 52ND AND 53RD STREETS)

The Seagram Building was the masterpiece of seventy-three-year-old Ludwig Mies van der Rohe, one of the greatest architects of that era, and fifty-year-old Philip Johnson, who would become one of America's premier architects. The building is an elegant curtain wall of bronze, tinted glass, and steel, and best captures the spirit of post-war America—sleek, modern, and forward-looking.

On the occasion of the hundredth anniversary of the Seagram & Sons Corporation, Samuel Bronfman, the company's board chairman, decided to erect a skyscraper in Manhattan on valuable Park Avenue property. Bronfman had a California firm, Luckman and Pereira, design the new building. Luckman had been the head of Lever Brothers and had commissioned Skidmore, Owings & Merrill to create the Lever House. Bronfman reasoned that Luckman would be a good person to oversee his project. When Bronfman's daughter, Phyllis Lambert, a student of architecture living in Paris, saw the plans, she made it clear that she was not pleased with the uninspired design. Bronfman was persuaded to turn over the entire project to his daughter.

Lambert asked a family friend, Alfred Barr, Jr., the Director of Collections of the Museum of Modern Art, for advice and he quickly arranged a meeting with Philip Johnson, the departing head of the museum's architecture department. Lambert and Johnson had some of world's leading architects submit plans: Eero Saarinen, Marcel Breuer, I.M. Pei, Frank Lloyd Wright, Le Corbusier, and Mies van der Rohe. Mies received the commission not only because he was the great modernist at the time but also because he had an even temperament and, unlike many architects, could work beyond his ego.

Quite unusual for a commission, the budget was enormous. Bronfman and Lambert understood the advantages of having the corporate name identified with a building. They wanted to create a sumptuous building that would represent not just their company, but, as Phyllis Lambert said, "be the crowning glory of everyone's work, his [Bronfman's] own, the contractor's, and Mies's." As history has revealed, the building turned out to be one of the most distinguished achievements of the age. The Seagram Building is a single slab of glass and bronze set back on a raised plaza running along Park Avenue. The thirty-eight-story tower has an uninterrupted curtain wall of bronze and a specially tinted glass (matching the Seagram's whiskey bottle) to give the building its luxurious look. The sides at the base are sheathed in granite, travertine, and imported marbles. These expensive materials gave the Seagram Building a richness unknown to other New York City skyscrapers.

The building was the first to be planned—inside and out—using a modular grid. Inside, all lighting, electrical services, and wall panels are modular, flexible, and moveable. Depending on the configuration, there could be vast spaces on a floor or small

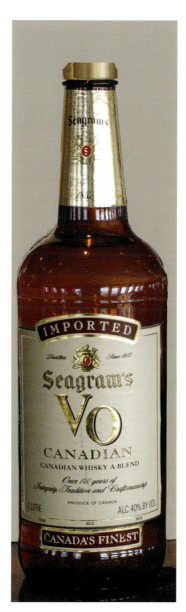

A bottle of Seagram's VO Canadian Whiskey.

Seagram Building | 69

compartments. All the windows are floor to ceiling and to ensure their harmony, the windows blinds have only three positions—fully opened, half open, fully closed--to endow the façade with uniformity.

Running up the side of the building are 4½ x 6 inch bronze I-beams. These continuous vertical elements have no structural purpose but are symbolic of the modern structure within and draw the eye upwards.

The single thirty-eight-story slab of the Seagram Building, together with the Lever House, mark a dramatic turn in the conception of the New York skyscraper. Although the 1916 Zoning Law which mandated setbacks was still in effect, that law allowed for a building to rise in one continuous block as long as the tower covered only a small percentage of the site, creating a public plaza. Taking advantage of this provision, these post-war buildings eschewed the traditional setbacks and chose this alternative, thereby changing the city skyline and also the experience of urban space below.

The plaza in front of the Seagram Building became a public space for all the workers on Park Avenue. The area was so unusual in the dense masonry of Park Avenue that it captivated the public's attention; people came here just to relax. The surface of the plaza is executed in pink granite and has two shallow reflecting pools. Next to the outer edges of the pools are greenish marble benches used by New Yorkers in good weather to chat and eat. The only asymmetrical element in the entire plaza is the bronze flagpole.

Philip Johnson was the person most responsible for the treatment of the interior. He designed the elevators, the lighting, and the lobby. The travertine marble employed at the base on the exterior was carried through to the entire lobby. Similarly, bronze fittings were used throughout the building. Even the elevator cabs were specially designed with stainless steel and bronze mesh panels. As is evident, Lambert provided a very generous budget for constructing the building.

A view into the lobby of the Seagram Building.

Indeed, the building was so costly, the New York Tax Commission taxed Seagram & Sons at a rate that was 50% higher than an ordinary building. The tax authorities reasoned that all the money spent on this building to make is so exceptional was taxable. Seagram & Sons went to court to contest the exorbitant tax rate and lost

The building had accouterments that today seem mundane but at the time were touted as the most efficient features that America could provide. For example, there was a bill changer, the first of its kind, that could change a dollar into ten dimes, four quarters, and other combinations. It was prophesied this machine would "usher in a new era in customer automation." Another innovation was an automatic timer that adjusted the lighting in the lobby to respond to the changing light of the day. On a bright day the lights dimmed automatically; on dark days, the lights became brighter. Whereas the elevators in most skyscrapers were manually operated by elevator boys, the Lever House had passenger-operated elevators. Automation was omnipresent and suggested that everything would be possible in a more efficient future.

The Four Seasons Restaurant, reached by an entrance on the 52nd Street side of the building, is one of the finest example of International Style interiors. Philip Johnson oversaw its design. This deluxe restaurant has a lower entrance lobby, two major dinning rooms, and small private dining rooms. Its décor, like its cuisine, is refined and sumptuous. The Mies van der Rohe seats, rich Brazilian rosewood paneling, Fortuny silk, and metallic curtains of gold, copper, and silver anodized aluminum beads contribute to the restrained but opulent effect.

A view of the exposed I-beams on the Seagram Building.

Pan Am Building
Architects: Emery Roth & Sons, Pietro Belluschi, and Walter Gropius, completed 1963
200 Park Avenue (between 45th and 47th Streets)

The Pan Am Building (presently MetLife) much celebrated as the world's largest office building when it was built, has become an emblem of all that is wrong with modern architecture. There is probably no building in Manhattan that is hated by the public as much as this behemoth. Indeed, in 1987, *New York Magazine* featured it on the cover being smashed by a wrecking ball and the headline, "The Buildings New Yorkers Love to Hate." Despite this negative assessment, it is a product of one of the world's great architects, Walter Gropius, and one of the most complex engineering projects of the age.

The 1916 Zoning Law was still in force and encouraged light streaming to the street but did little to break up the dense urban structure. The Lever House and Seagram Buildings tried to forge new architectural and urban planning frontiers but had few followers at first.

New York Central Railroad owned Grand Central Terminal, as well as some of the choicest real estate in the center of Manhattan: forty-eight acres between 42nd and 50th Streets and bounded by Lexington and Madison Avenues. In 1954, Robert Young, the new chairman of the railroad, knew the time was right to develop this area and relieve the company of its significant debt. Knocking down the venerable Grand Central station was very much part of the plan until such strong objections came from so many areas that Young could no longer move forward. Instead, he conceived of building over and around the historic terminal, and after much political intrigue, Emery Roth & Sons was engaged to build a massive office complex there.

Emery Roth & Sons was an old New York firm, established almost a century before. In the 1920s, Emery Roth was responsible for some of New York's most elegant high-rise apartment buildings in the Beaux-Arts style. Roth's sons, Richard and Julian, continued their father's firm but abandoned the old-fashioned look of historicism for a modern, progressive style. Rather than adopting the lessons of Gordon Bunshaft, Mies van der Rohe, or Philip Johnson, they built wedding cake modernist buildings–following the 1916 laws concerning setbacks but cloaking them in modernist garb. As they so aptly said, no money was wasted on ornamentation—historical or modern.

In 1958, to aid them on this project, Emery Roth & Sons called upon Walter Gropius and Pietro Belluschi to help create a "more aesthetic" building design. The reasoning was that an artist-architect would create a quality building and bring quality clients. Richard Roth was the one who suggested Gropius, a former dean of architecture at Harvard, and Belluschi, dean of architecture at MIT. Roth hoped that the two giants would be very busy with their other work and not get too involved in the New York project. He wanted their names but not their interference.

Gropius and Belluschi had other ideas. They did not want their names attached to a less-than-distinguished building of the type that Roth was usually known for. They agreed to proceed but with very clear conditions. Specifically, they would withdraw their names if they were not in agreement with the final product. The news of their appointment created positive publicity and excitement in the world of Manhattan architecture.

Walter Gropius was the high priest of architecture. While with the Bauhaus in Weimar and Dessau, he became a leading spokesman for modernism in architecture. As a refugee fleeing the Nazis, he brought his progressive ideas to America and, as the dean of architecture at Harvard, to a premier center of higher education in the United States. Similarly, Pietro Belluschi had fled

A helicopter taking off from the Pan Am Building in the 1960s.

the totalitarian restrictions of Mussolini for the United States. He set up a very successful practice in Portland, Oregon, designing modernist houses, churches, and commercial buildings. In 1950, he was appointed the dean of MIT's school of architecture—another of this country's premier schools for architecture and engineering. Gropius was a political mover and shaker; Belluschi was a brilliant loner. The two artist-architects could not be further apart.

The team of Gropius, Belluschi, and Roth faced many hurdles. Roth was responsible for interior spaces and all working drawings, while Gropius and Belluschi oversaw all public spaces and the exterior. The building design emerged as an eight-story base with a fifty-six-story tower. While Gropius and Belluschi wanted quality, Roth always sought a more economical path. For example, the artist-architects wanted rounded columns in the lobby while Roth insisted on less expensive square ones. The lobby ended up with square ones. Finance usually overruled taste. One notable exception was the special prefabricated concrete panels chosen for the exterior skin. These panels, known as Mo-Sai because of their mosaic appearance, weighed far more than the builders had planned and were difficult to place into position, a problem which was only overcome at great expense. Worse, the company making the panels went bankrupt during the project.

Pan Am, the great American international airline, signed on as the major tenant but with conditions. Above all, it insisted on having its name displayed on all façades of the building. Gropius rejected this idea, saying this would be overkill, and agreed only to it being displayed on the two main sides—north and south—and just the logo of the Pan Am globe on the short sides. This arrangement was accepted by all parties.

Criticism of the building's design started immediately. The earliest detractors complained that "the building was an offense, sociologically, aesthetically, and ideologically." People were worried about the damage that would be done by adding the world's largest office building to this already dense area. Ada Louise Huxtable, the great critic of the *New York Times*, asked, "Marvel or Monster?" Despite the great names involved, she thought that this project would end up poorly. As the building was rising, the debate increased in strength. When it officially opened on March 7, 1963, pointedly neither Gropius nor Belluschi were in attendance. On the other hand, it boosted the reputation of Emery Roth & Sons because it showed the company could erect a skyscraper.

As tenants were moving into the building, criticism from home and abroad continued to mount. It was too big and ugly, unresponsive to the city around it, inappropriate, and above all, it destroyed the vista down Park Avenue and overwhelmed the site. Belluschi retired from his seat as dean at MIT and never acknowledged the building. Gropius was blamed for the design and the negative comments the building received. When he died in 1969, the Pan Am Building was seen as the low point of his otherwise stellar career.

By 1980, Pan Am's fortune was fading. The building was put up for sale and Metropolitan Life Insurance Company bought it as an investment for only $400 million. The Pan Am sign remained on the building until 1992, well after the airline went bankrupt. When the insurance company announced a change of signage, people protested. Although New Yorkers hated the building, they had become accustomed to it. Even Jacqueline Kennedy Onassis wanted the sign saved, and the Landmark Commission considered designating the hated building a historic monument to keep the Pan Am signage, but that move failed. Ultimately, Metropolitan Life Insurance Company removed the sign and replaced it with its own giant logo.

The Pan Am Building looming over the façade of the Grand Central Terminal in the 1960s.

World Trade Center
Architects: Minoru Yamasaki with Emery Roth & Sons, completed primarily in 1970-71, other buildings 1975-87
An area bounded by Liberty, Church, Vesey, and West Streets

The world paused on a bright, sunny Tuesday in September 2001 when two planes commandeered by terrorists destroyed the gigantic Twin Towers, a symbol of Western capitalism. The World Trade Center was actually a complex of seven buildings in lower Manhattan, but the North and South Tower were the most famous. The Twin Towers, as they were affectionately called, were 110 floors each and reigned as the world's tallest buildings from 1971 to 1973. They were home to 430 companies from twenty-eight countries, and accommodated 50,000 workers each day.

The project to create this mammoth complex of world trade had its roots a half a century years earlier. In February 1955, one of New York City's boldest developers, William Zeckendorf, proposed a great building complex to David Rockefeller, a senior vice-president at Chase Manhattan Bank and the youngest son of John D. Rockefeller, Jr., the man who built Rockefeller Center. This development was aimed at keeping the headquarters of the great bank in lower Manhattan and not moving to a new location in the increasingly popular midtown area, especially along Park Avenue. Zeckendorf proposed that they should build a grand skyscraper to accommodate all the bank's offices. Rockefeller agreed to this bold plan, which would inject new vitality into the Wall Street area. David Rockefeller, chairman of the Downtown-Lower Manhattan Association, started planning for a great complex dedicated to making New York City the center of world trade and finance. In January 1960, Rockefeller and city and state officials selected thirteen acres of land along the East River for this grand project.

Essential to the success of such a massive project was securing tremendous financial resources and obtaining the land. Rockefeller knew that he had to persuade the bi-state Port Authority of New York and New Jersey to adopt the project as its own. In the late 1950s, the Port Authority was flush with cash, and it had the power of eminent domain to procure a great amount of land. With little coaxing, the Port Authority adopted the project. Combining political savvy, cunning skill, and amazing luck, Austin Tobin, the chairman of the Authority, and his team were able to goad the two state governors, state legislators, and city authorities to approve the massive plan—but not without many compromises. The primary concession to the New Jersey officials was to take over an outdated, bankrupt rail link for New Jersey commuters and to relocate the complex to the west side of Manhattan facing the Garden State. To benefit New York City, Tobin and his team renegotiated the relationship of the Port Authority with the city. In particular, it secured an agreement to use the excess fill from the project to create twenty-three acres of new land called Battery Park City.

A view of Radio Row in the 1930s.

Another major challenge for Tobin was to overcome a series of lawsuits from neighborhood merchants. The local business owners claimed that the seizure of their land was unconstitutional as this was a private-public project and there was no public purpose. The challenge wound its way through the court system and although the Port Authority won in some courts, it lost in others. In the end, it won the only argument that mattered, in the United States Supreme Court. With concessions in hand and lawsuits overcome, some ten years after the first idea crossed Rockefeller's desk, the project finally moved ahead in the late summer of 1966.

The commission to design the massive project went to a rather unknown, unassuming Michigan-based architect of Japanese ancestry, Minoru Yamasaki. He was aided by the quintessential New York architectural firm of Emery Roth & Sons. Tobin rejected the great architects of the time—Gordon Bunshaft at SOM, Wallace K. Harrison, Walter Gropius, Philip Johnson, I.M. Pei, and Louis Khan. Yamasaki had never built a major skyscraper and was actually afraid of heights. Nor had he previously worked in New York City. Yamasaki was a disciple of the International Style but Tobin knew he was not idealistic and beholden to it. He was primarily an engineer with a sixth sense of building dynamics. Most importantly for the Port Authority, he was client-oriented and was not a celebrity architect whose personality would dominate the project.

The design of the two principal towers was sparse and innovative. Each was a square with four equal sides, and was sheathed with a latticework of steel. Most remarkable, this external steel skeleton was weight-bearing—one of the first buildings built in a century which rejected an internal skeletal superstructure. This allowed each floor to be open, uninterrupted by supporting columns. At the base, Yamasaki used ten-story high Gothic arches, the only decorative elements on the buildings. Rather than having massive floor-to-ceiling windows to take advantage of the grand vistas, Yamasaki designed very narrow, eighteen-inch wide windows in a pseudo-Gothic shape. Afraid of heights, the architect constrained the size of the windows to make everyone inside feel secure.

A major problem facing Yamasaki and his team was getting the thousands of workers up and down the 110 floors in the giant structures. The area normally needed for adequate elevator banks would have significantly reduced valuable rental space. Using the New York subway system of local and express trains, Yamasaki adopted a plan of local and express elevators connected by sky lobbies. Dedicated express elevators went from the lobby to the 48th and 78th floors where passengers switched to locals. It was a devilishly simple solution that had never been tried before and was an instant success.

Yamasaki's design for two 110-story buildings left no critic mute. Some hailed the neo-Gothic latticework of the weight-bearing façade as genius. Some saw the two towers as giant minimalist sculptures playing off against each other, while other writers, more critical, described them as just two giant office filing cabinets. Various critics claimed that they had no relevance to the tradition of stately New York skyscrapers. Worse, they stood apart from the

The lobby of the World Trade Center.

city and especially the neighborhood in which they were located. The management sadly moved all "human" services—restaurants, shops, and food outlets to the various sub-basements of the towers leaving the great plaza a dead, soulless space.

Despite these flaws, real or imagined, the buildings were embraced by the public and quickly entered into their imagination. They attracted entertainers and daredevils. In 1974, Philippe Petit, the French high-wire artist, "conquered" the buildings by surreptitiously putting 450-pound cable between the two towers and then walking and dancing between the buildings for forty-five minutes. In 1976 the buildings were used by Hollywood as the setting for the remake of *King Kong,* replacing the Empire State Building, the focus of the original 1933 film. Within six years of the opening, their popularity was secure.

Visitors came in droves. The 107th floor of the South Tower held an enclosed observation deck. The public flocked to look south over New York Harbor and were fascinated to watch helicopters flying below them. The 107th floor in the North Tower housed the popular Windows on the World Restaurant. There was also an extremely popular public bar, The Greatest Bar on Earth. The food was reviewed to be very good but the space was known as having the best wine cellar in New York.

Despite the lack of critical acclaim among architectural professionals, the public was captivated by the gigantic size of the buildings. They became the symbol of America and the West. As symbols, they became targets of fanatics. In February 1993, terrorists detonated a truck bomb in the basement garage of the Towers. Six people died and the attack caused $510,000,000 in damages. Once repaired, the Towers were reopened, but under heightened security. On September 11, 2001, fanatics associated with Al Qaeda hijacked two Boeing 767 airliners and flew them deliberately into the Towers. The resulting fire and subsequent collapse of both buildings claimed almost 3,000 lives. Investigations into why the towers imploded on themselves concluded that the steel could not stand up to the immense inferno created by the jet fuel. The report also remarked that it was a miracle that the buildings stood as long as they did and allowed over 15,000 people to escape. The consequences of the tragedy of September 11, 2001, forever changed the way tall buildings are conceived and constructed.

The windows of 2 World Trade Center at lobby level.

American Telephone & Telegraph Building
Architects: Philip Johnson and John Burgee with Harry Simmons, completed 1983
550 Madison Avenue (between 55th and 56th Streets)

Clad in pink granite, ornamented with giant arches, portholes, and columns, and topped by a dramatic broken pediment 660 feet above Madison Avenue, the 1983 American Telephone and Telegraph Building (presently the Sony Building) transformed the New York skyline and changed the direction of late twentieth-century architectural history. Built as the world headquarters of AT&T, America's giant telecommunication company, it is a tower of only thirty-seven stories, although the zoning law could have permitted a tower of sixty stories. One of the great names of modernism, Philip Johnson totally rejected the tradition of an unornamented vertical slab and glass curtain wall to return to traditional building materials and historical ornamentation. What caused such a design shift? How could someone who championed the founders of modernism such as Walter Gropius and Mies van der Rohe, now move in this new direction?

AT&T had outgrown its lower Manhattan headquarters which had served the company well for sixty-seven years. Twenty architectural firms were invited to submit designs for a new building. Although Johnson and John Burgee were asked to submit a bid, through a clerical error they did not. When they realized their mistake as well as the scale of the project, they hurriedly put together a minimal proposal. They made it to the short list and when they were interviewed, they brought with them only two illustrations—their Seagram and Pennzoil Buildings—as well as lots of experience and charm. Miraculously, they were selected.

The primary charge to the architects from the AT&T board was that the building had to be a world-class skyscraper representing their company and had to be as iconic as the Seagram Building. Johnson and Burgee, along with Harry Simmons, knew that a modernist glass curtain wall building would not do; they needed to reinvent the concept of a skyscraper for their clients.

Philip Johnson had been a leading champion of the International Style since the 1930s. His post-war buildings such as his Glass House in New Caanan, Connecticut, and his work with Mies on the Seagram Building proved how stylish modernism could be. As the 1960s and '70s came around, he slowly shed his modernist roots for a more eclectic style. His late 1950s design for the New York State Theater in Lincoln Center reveals how he began to embrace classical forms and ornament—albeit in a restrained and minimalist way. In 1967, Johnson took an architectural partner half his age, John Burgee. The Johnson and Burgee

A view in the public space of the AT&T Building.

architectural team flourished, as it pushed architectural frontiers. Among their many projects were Pennzoil Place in Houston and Crystal Cathedral in Garden Grove, California, where Gothic towers rose in a novel, Post-Modernist vocabulary.

The design of the AT&T Building rejects entirely the modernist approach of one solid slab and harks back to the early twentieth century when the skyscraper was conceived as a tripartite division of base, shaft, and capital. It is clad in roughly finished pink Stony Creek granite, the same stone used for Grand Central Station and the preferred building material of early Beaux-Arts structures in New York City. The 131 foot-tall base is pierced by arches on all sides. The Madison Avenue front has a monumental central arch, flanked by columns rising over a covered loggia. It is more akin to a McKim, Mead & White building of 1912 than to a 1980s Madison Avenue construction, except that the scale is colossal.

The most distinguishing and controversial feature of the building is the uppermost portion, which is a massive broken pediment rising thirty feet above the last story. This dramatic feature likens the building to a giant Chippendale highboy or a massive eighteenth-century grandfather clock. Johnson had planned that steam would emerge out of the building, from the midpoint of the broken pediment. When lit at night, it would create a dramatic, theatrical sight--something belonging to an imaginary scheme of Étienne-Louis Boullée in the late eighteenth century.

So unusual was the design of the AT&T Building that the *New York Times* featured it on the front page of its newspaper when it was announced. It drew both damnation and praise. Perhaps the strongest negative judgment came from the critic Michael Sorkin who wrote in his book, *Exquisite Corpse*, "...The building sucks. ... it is graceless and same old." At the other extreme, the *New York Times* critic Paul Goldberger praised the design, opining that it was a "Major Monument of Post-Modernism." Was the AT&T building a failure or pure genius? Looking back on it with the perspective of thirty years, even if it was not the first Post-Modern building, it nonetheless defined this architectural style and it announced in no uncertain way that the sparse, clean look of 1950s modernism was dead.

A detail of the model of the AT&T Building.

The elevation of the AT&T Building compared to a Chippendale-style grandfather clock.

Condé Nast Building
Architects: Fox & Fowle, completed 1999
4 Times Square (42nd Street and Broadway)

After a fifteen-year hiatus in the construction of tall buildings in New York City, Foxe & Fowle, working for the Durst Corporation, undertook a new forty-eight-story building, named after its chief tenant, the publishing house Condé Nast. That led the way to a building revival in New York City at the start of the new millennium. Soon after Condé Nast committed to taking a third of the building, the law firm Skadden, Arps, Meagher & Flom took 40% of it, making the prospective structure a success before it was even built.

Fox & Fowle championed both new technologies and high-style design in their building. The challenge facing the architects was to marry the staid and dignified look of the corporate headquarters of the two main tenants on 42nd Street with the glitzy spirit needed on the Times Square façade.

Fox & Fowle was celebrating its twentieth anniversary when the Condé Nast building was under construction. They were a New York City firm whose philosophy was to build well-designed, high quality buildings that fit comfortably into their urban context. Their buildings were not necessarily flashy but they were always good neighbors. For example, the Seaport Tower at 40 Fulton Street, an office building executed in 1986, is a twenty-nine-story building that fits perfectly into the seaport area.

The Condé Nast Building does not appear to be one solid tower but, instead, seems to be divided into two distinct zones. It is a Janus-like building with two façades, each with a different personality. Facing 42nd Street, the façade of the corporate offices is formal and understated, and is sheathed in granite. On Times Square, the glass-fronted façade ends with a large turret housing the NASDAQ electronic ticker, displayed on one of the world's largest video screens. The screen plays colorful, animated videos and dramatic still images. To let light into the offices behind it, the screen is punctuated with windows.

The top of the building changed the skyline of New York. It functions as a "hat truss," transferring the stress from one side of the building to the other, but it also serves as a striking crown. It is a strange agglomeration of a tower with rounded corners overlaid by four skeletal structures carrying seventy-foot square super-sign armatures. Originally, these armatures were to have carried advertising. Also, poking out with great gusto are girders, pipes, and other construction features. The *New York Times* critic, Herbert Muschamp, wrote that the crown resembles "high technology hardware popping out of the top." It is very much in the Russian Constructivist mode of the 1920s, quite unlike the solid structures normally found on skyscrapers. With mixed media, differently textured stone, and flashing LED signage, the spirit of Post-Modernism is very much present in the Condé Nast building.

More importantly for skyscraper design, Durst Corporation asked Fox & Fowle to create a building that would be environmentally friendly. The greening of the skyscraper was in its infancy when the Condé Nast building was conceived.

The Hat Truss of the Condé Nast Building.

Many critics claim that all high-rise building are nothing more than "energy-hungry parasites" in the urban landscape and, indeed, many consider a green skyscraper to be a contradiction in terms. Certainly it was a daunting task to conceive of an environmentally friendly high-rise building in the 1980s, but there were sound reasons for building green. Beyond being kind to the environment, building green meant cheaper running costs.

The major obstacle was that Fox & Fowle were not trained in applied ecology. Thus the architects approached the task of greening a skyscraper in a multi-disciplinary way. They assembled a large team of consultants from disparate fields: government agencies, conservation groups, power companies, and think tanks. The team settled on a number of ideas: creative recirculation of fresh air far above the minimum standards required by code, chutes for recyclable paper waste and provision for storage of the waste at the loading docks, occupancy sensors for adjusting light and services, and high performance glass curtain walls that produce energy. The most important advancement was the building's energy systems. The team considered wind turbines, gas turbines, thermal storage, and other methods, but settled on the use of photovoltaic and fuel cells. They were used here for the first time in a high-rise building. The final plan of eight 200-kilowatt fuel cells was never achieved, but the two which went on line gave the industry a model for future green buildings.

The 42nd Street entrance to the Condé Nast Building.

The Times Square façade of the Condé Nast Building.

Westin New York at Times Square
Architect: Arquitectonica, completed 2002
270 West 43rd Street (at Eighth Avenue)

In the 1960s and '70s, rampant prostitution, open buying and selling of drugs, and the expanding number of pornography cinemas and stores in Times Square and the immediate area encompassing The Great White Way was an embarrassment to New York City. Successive mayors of New York tried to clean up the area but to no avail. From the mid-1970s onward, the city made this midtown area, including Times Square, a special zone hoping they could ban or displace pornography and reclaim the area. It was not until the beginning of the 1980s under Mayor Ed Koch that the transformation began. With approval of the New York City government, developers razed whole sections of the 42nd Street area, including some historically significant buildings and theaters, to make way for new buildings. Much to the consternation of New Yorkers, the plans had the Disney Corporation taking part in the rejuvenation of Times Square. The thought of the disneyfication of the area was upsetting to many.

Catty-cornered from the main bus terminal in New York City, the area around what would be the Westin Hotel was busy with commuters coming and going, passing by rows of pornographic movie houses, hordes of the homeless, and drug addicts. As an entryway to 42nd Street, the planned hotel was to serve as an anchor to the western end of the entire project, and therefore had to make a significant statement.

Robert A. M. Stern, the dean of the Architecture School at Yale University, chaired a committee to set the guidelines that would govern all new buildings in the area. The requirements included the dramatic use of billboards and especially neon lights. The New Times Square was to be a place where graphic design and architecture came together. Four firms submitted proposals for the new hotel complex, each linked to a different hotel chain: Frank Gehry with Disney Corporation and Westin Hotel; Eisemann Architects was with the Hilton Corporation; Hahn and Venturi with Marriott; and William Tabler with Milestein properties. Over the course of the project, the Miami-based firm of Arquitectonica replaced Frank Gehry, while Michael Graves and Zaha Hadid replaced Venturi. The

A view of the stores in the E-Walk along 42nd Street.

Westin Hotel | 89

project was awarded to the Westin Hotel and Arquitectonica, but Disney had dropped out of the project entirely.

There is no other building like the Westin Hotel in the skyline of New York. The structure is divided into three sections: a four-story retail podium, a nine-story mid-level rise, and a tower. Along 42nd Street is the retail podium called E-Walk, which is a series of street-level retail stores and restaurants designed by D'Agostino Izzo Quirk Architects. E-Walk gives the illusion of a series of separate small spaces that are buried in a mass of billboards and flashing electric signs. It is visually rich and distracting.

Growing out of E-Walk is a mid-level rise of nine-stories designed by Arquitectonica. This volume is earth-toned and the walls are meant to look like an origami box unfolded. Visually, it is meant to remind us of both an earth outcropping, such as is found in Central Park, as well as a giant meteor which has crashed into 42nd Street—a humorous theme to the building.

Resting on the nine-story mid-level rise is the main tower of the hotel also by Arquitectonica. This is divided into two unequal zones, meant to remind us of glass prisms. Each side is decorated differently: one has vertical panels colored a silvery-blue, and the other horizontal panels colored bronze. Interspersed throughout are stripes of brilliant color—purple, blue, rust, and turquoise. The effect of the glass surfaces makes the colored panels shimmer as the weather and light conditions change throughout the day. This polychromatic treatment of the tower's exterior walls is certainly more Latin and Miami-oriented than is normally found in New York City.

Between the two zones is a dramatic curving shaft of light. It originates in the "Earth" base, runs over the surface of the tower, and the powerful beam shoots into the night sky. It produces a light show par excellence. Overall, the Westin Hotel is a giant sculpture and pure theater. It is glitzy and kitsch, meant to capture the viewer's imagination and attention.

Right from the beginning, the reviews of the building were very critical. At the time, almost every reviewer invoked the word "ugly." John Gardner called it the ugliest building in the city. Paul Goldberger thought it the ugliest curtain wall in the city, and most thought it marred the New York City skyline. Only one reviewer, Herbert Muschamp, thought it was appropriate for its location. No matter what, Arquitectonica with its Latin American-inspired architecture had arrived in the Big Apple.

A view of the mid-level rise of the Westin Hotel. Facing page: The Westin Hotel at night.

Westin Hotel

Time Warner Center
Architect: David Childs for Skidmore, Owings & Merrill, completed 2004
10 Columbus Circle (at 59th Street and Broadway)

For generations, conventioneers to New York City descended on the Coliseum at Columbus Circle, whether to visit the annual boat and auto shows, or America's largest college fair. Ultimately this building proved too small, and a decision was made to replace it with a new convention center below 34th Street, the Jacob Javits Convention Center, which opened in 1986. The previous year, the Metropolitan Transit Authority, the organization that runs New York's subways and busses and which owned the Coliseum, put the parcel of land up for sale. It was the largest plot of land in the city to be offered in a half-century, and was well situated, just below Lincoln Center. Interest in developing the 2.5 million square feet was great. Thirteen developers submitted proposals.

Many of the major architects in the United States bid on the project: Michael Graves, I.M. Pei, César Pelli, Kevin Roche, Moshe Safdie, Skidmore, Owings & Merrill, are but a few who submitted plans. The designs ranged from what would have been the world's largest building at 137 stories to a plan that incorporated the existing 1950s building into the design. The winning design was by Moshe Safdie. According to newspaper reports, it "… looked more like Buck Rogers" and did not fit into the tradition of New York skyscrapers. Criticism poured in from all quarters. Despite the problems, the city of New York approved the project.

Opponents of the Safdie project included New York's rich and famous. Jacqueline Kennedy Onassis, joined by Bill Moyers, objected that the bulky project would block sunlight into Central Park. I.M. Pei thought it impractical. As is often the case where there are opposing interests, the project ended up in the New York State Supreme Court. Much to the astonishment of the public, the court voided the sale of the Coliseum site and the entire project was on the verge of collapse.

Mayor Ed Koch saved the day by boldly replacing Moshe Safdie with David Childs of Skidmore, Owings & Merrill. The SOM project was more conservative and fit much better into the fabric of Columbus Circle. The new plan was approved in 1989 by the city authorities.

Delays plagued the project in the 1990s, the New York real estate market collapsed, and the entire project was suspended. Throughout the late 1990s, various schemes were put forth. In 1997, Mayor Rudolph Giuliani held the project hostage unless some major

public component was included. To overcome that formidable hurdle, a grand 2000-seat hall was included to house *Jazz at Lincoln Center*. In September 1999, the old Coliseum was demolished and finally, after fifteen years of delays, a new building began to rise under the direction of David Childs and SOM.

The Time Warner Center is a mixed-use, high-rise building with offices (mostly occupied by Time Warner), residential apartments, the Mandarin Oriental Hotel, an upscale shopping mall, high-class restaurants and bars, a theater for jazz, television studios for CNN, and a massive parking garage. A large supermarket, Whole Foods Market, occupies the entire basement.

Fronting the complex is a seven-story shopping center that curves to correspond to Columbus Circle. Behind are two "bases"—one twenty stories, the other twenty-four; rising from the bases are two setback towers. To meet the objection of the local communities, the height of the towers was capped at fifty-three floors. The curtain wall exterior is dark glass and at the top are large vertical fins recalling 1930s apartment houses on Central Park West. The outline of the building in the New York City skyline marks the northernmost portion of midtown Manhattan. However, while continuing the tradition of the post-war skyscraper, the many intersecting planes create a dynamic, prismatic building typical of the twenty-first century.

The towers of the Time Warner Center after a storm.

Time Warner Center | 93

HEARST TOWER
ARCHITECT: NORMAN FOSTER OF FOSTER + PARTNERS, COMPLETED 2006
300 WEST 57TH STREET (AT EIGHTH AVENUE)

The Hearst Tower, "the Greenest Skyscraper in the World," was eight decades in the making. In the 1920s, the publishing magnate William Randolph Hearst wanted to build his new office headquarters, the International Magazine Building, in the middle of what he predicted would be a vibrant media and cultural neighborhood. Carnegie Hall at 57th Street and Sixth Avenue anchored one end, and the Metropolitan Opera House was planned for Columbus Circle at the other end. In 1928, Hearst commissioned the Viennese-born architect and theater set designer, Joseph Urban, to create a headquarters that would fit into this developing artsy area. His structure was conceived as in-city stage sets with four entrances on three sides of the building. The allegorical sculptures of Music, Art, Comedy, Tragedy, Sport, Industry, Printing, and Science, were intended to reflect Hearst's vision of the varied cultural activities he foresaw for the area. Only the base was built and it was unusually sturdy because a grand tower was always planned to rise up on top of it. The onset of the Depression, followed closely by World War II, halted any thought of expanding the building and, additionally, plans had long been abandoned to relocate the opera house to this area. By 2001, the Hearst Empire had grown considerably with 2000 employees spread in different offices throughout Manhattan. The time had come, as William Randolph Hearst had envisioned in 1926, to consolidate everyone under one roof.

The commission for the Hearst Tower was awarded to Norman Foster, one of Britain's most prolific, creative, and award-winning architects. Foster, who had never designed a New York City building, had to join Urban's Art Deco base with something new and evocative. Prior to the Hearst Tower, Foster's successes were many but especially noteworthy were the HSBC Main Building in Hong Kong, Commerzbank Tower in Frankfurt, and the Great Court of the British Museum in London.

An important meeting between Hearst officials and Foster + Partners to present the tower was on September 12, 2001—the day after the fall of the Twin Towers. The meeting was cancelled and reconvened four weeks later. With the fires still smoldering at Ground Zero, the relationship between the city and tall buildings had changed forever. The board of the Hearst Corporation had to decide whether even to continue to build a skyscraper given the horrific events of one month earlier, and Foster + Partners had to quickly consider security in a post-9/11 world. The building was approved by the Hearst Board and Foster + Partners adjusted its

A view of the original Hearst Building by Joseph Urban, c.1930.

designs for added security in the newly changed building climate.

Foster encouraged the Hearst Corporation to adopt an environmentally responsible philosophy for its company. He advocated that their new building should be sustainable and should adopt the latest green technology. The Hearst Tower is also one of the rare examples in the history of New York City skyscrapers where an entire building was commissioned by one company for its exclusive use. Most companies have occupied only a part of their building and leased the rest out as commercial space, thus often creating a need to maximize rental space. Having an owner-occupied building allowed Foster creative freedom to design a space that was both inventive and user-friendly, and he did not have to worry about the client's need to exploit valuable rental space.

Foster designed a forty-story tower growing out of the Urban six-story base. Foster never thought the Urban building was architecturally interesting but as the 1929 building was landmarked by the City of New York, he could not alter its exterior. Rather, he gutted the interior, recycling 80% of the material, and his tower rose from within. Striking is Foster's exterior of crisscrossing stainless steel bars forming a diagonal grid or a "diagrid." Indeed, there are no vertical steel beams used above the base, a first for an American skyscraper. Foster's diagrid interlocks recycled stainless steel beams to create triangular shaped areas with diagonal support beams using 21% less steel than would be required on a standard steel-framed building. Foster took great care in leveraging the triangular design by creating special cut-away corners on each level of the building, called Birds Mouths, which afford great vistas onto the city. Foster wanted these special, well-lit, and open areas to be public spaces for conferences and waiting areas, so that the majority of the Hearst employees could experience the city. He particularly did not want workers looking into dark corners. The most impressive interior is the three-story sky-lit atrium at the main entrance. Reached by a dramatic escalator, the atrium serves as cafeteria, café, and general meeting area. Surrounding the escalators are waterfalls, *Ice Falls*, which are both beautiful and practical, as they cool in the summer and humidify in the winter. Greeting the visitor at the top of the waterfalls is Richard Long's monumental mural, *River Lines*, constructed of earth from the nearby Hudson River and Long's native Avon River.

There are many "green" aspects to the building. Almost all the materials used in construction of the building were made from recycled material,

A view of the lobby of the Hearst Tower, showing how Foster's structure is joined to Urban's base.

including 90% of the steel. Most of the interior materials, such as the carpets and woods, were locally sourced. The building uses 26% less energy than the minimum normally needed for a structure of this scale. A giant tank in the basement collects all rainwater, and that water is recycled to cool or humidify the lobby. Specially coated glass is used to let in the sunlight and at the same time keep out radiant heat. This is essential in New York's hot summers. Special tubes run in the floor for heating and cooling. Sensors throughout the building work to save electricity and water.

Aptly, one scholar described the Hearst Tower as a "Jack in the Box"—a surprise popping out of a standard box. This building and its diagrids add a distinctive note to the New York City skyline. Foster's edifice breaks with the strict, box-like symmetry of most New York City buildings but it fits comfortably into the urban fabric. It also marks the new direction for environmentally conscious skyscrapers.

The allegorical figure of *Tragedy* on the exterior of Urban's base. A view of the escalator going to the atrium of Foster's building, showing also the *Ice Falls* and Richard Long's mural.

NEW YORK TIMES BUILDING
Architect: Renzo Piano Building Workshop with FXFOWLE, completed 2007
620 Eighth Avenue (between 40th and 41st Streets)

By the millennium, *The New York Times*, America's most venerable newspaper, had outgrown its neo-Gothic, century-old building on 43rd Street just off of Times Square. Much to the surprise of New Yorkers, the newspaper's management decided to move its headquarters to a seedy area on Eighth Avenue, just opposite the Port Authority Bus Terminal and on the edge of the 42nd Street Redevelopment Project.

Four of the world's greatest architects sought the project: Norman Foster from England, Renzo Piano from Italy, and two American entrants, César Pelli, and a high-powered team of Frank Gehry and David Childs of Skidmore, Owings & Merrill. The designs were as varied as the architects. The façade of Foster's building was set at a right angle to Eighth Avenue, with greenery hanging off balconies of a sloping building. Piano proposed a traditional glass tower but which then was sheathed with sun- and heat-louvered screens. Pelli offered a massive tower rising up out of the urban fabric. The design favored by the developers and critics was Gehry and Childs/SOM's forty-five-story tower that was wrapped in what appeared to be billowing curtains of glass, the wall undulating as one would expect from Gehry. Their award-winning design would have changed the nature of skyscrapers in Manhattan, but suddenly Gehry and Childs withdrew from the project and the entire scheme was turned over to Renzo Piano, with the locally based firm of FXFOWLE Architects as partners.

Piano's building rises forty-seven stories above a five-story base. It is a rather traditional glass curtain façade which has a sunscreen of 250,000 white ceramic rods, each about $1^{5}/_{8}$ inches in diameter. The veil of ceramic tubes is set $1^{1}/_{2}$ feet out from the glass wall. The rods are organized so that workers have unobstructed views of the city yet are hidden from passersby in the street. However, the corners of the building are not covered with the screen of ceramic rods, and this unobscured glass allows a view of people moving up and down stairs.

The lobby is light, airy, and inviting, welcoming the pedestrian off the street. Upon entering the soaring lobby, the visitor looks past the elevator banks to a living green forest and to an auditorium beyond. It is a harmonious mixing of natural and man-made, and gives the effect of a Japanese garden with wall-less spaces. It is an amazing achievement within a skyscraper.

The chief tenant is the New York Times Company, which occupies half the building. The other half is given over to rentals--now occupied by law, architectural, and advertising firms. There are ground-floor retail stores as well.

Like many twenty-first-century skyscrapers, this building is designed to be green. Natural light filters in through the specially tinted glass walls. The ceramic rods, although decorative, block the direct light to reduce cooling and heating loads. The window shades are controlled by sensors that make them rise and descend as the ambient light changes. At the same time, the 18,000 dimmable, fluorescent fixtures are constantly being adjusted. Heat is recycled throughout the building while air circulation under the floor air reduces cooling needs. When weather conditions permit, cool, outside air is brought into the building to provide both cooling and fresh air. Urinals are waterless. The building was constructed without a parking garage to encourage employees and visitors to take public transportation or to use the specially built interior bicycle racks inside the building. The building is a marvel of green design.

A view from the cafeteria in the New York Times Building, showing the screen of ceramic rods.

New York by Gehry
Architect: Frank Gehry, completed 2011
8 Spruce Street (off of Park Row)

With its seventy-six stories and 901 units, no residential tower in New York City (or in the Western hemisphere) is taller than Frank Gehry's 8 Spruce Street. It is also the famed architect's first skyscraper.

Gehry defined the late Post-Modernist field of Deconstructivism. From the Guggenheim Museum in Bilbao to the Walt Disney Concert Hall in Los Angeles, Gehry has pushed the limits of how we think about architecture, with undulating walls, off-balanced towers, and gravity-defying roofs. No work defines Gehry as well as the Guggenheim Museum in Bilbao, Created in 1997, the flexible walls of titanium, glass, and limestone appear to explode and break away from the structure. His museum challenges the notion of a building, which normally is supposed to be stable and rational.

This same architectural personality is wholly reflected in New York by Gehry, which is dressed in a crumpled stainless steel skin. From afar, the profile of the building fits well into the New York skyline as a relatively traditional tower with classic setbacks. Up close, its shiny steel skin transforms the building as if its exterior were rippled and furrowed by running water. The surface undulates and shifts like Bernini's baroque sculpture, a particular love of Gehry's. He wanted the building to counteract the standardization of the corporate world, as represented by the boxy buildings on Wall Street. The architect believes that the world is not and should not be regular and standardized.

Gehry is the master at applying technology to his designs. Using specially designed computer software, he created the plans for the façade's 10,500 individual panels. Although fabricating them might normally have gone over budget, Permasteelisa, an Italian company, produced the panels at a reasonable price. Gehry also wanted the windows to undulate with the walls but that cost was too great. Nonetheless, the curvilinear façade enabled the architect to give each apartment bay windows with breathtaking views.

Up close, the building has some conservative, almost out-of-place aspects. Oddly, the south façade, facing downtown, is totally flat. Gehry explained that he needed one face of the building to be more regular to tone down the drama. Some critics have put forward the argument that this side faces Wall Street and the financial center of Manhattan which requires a conservative aspect. Also, the tower sits atop a fairly traditional, six-story red-orange brick base which is an elementary school. No distractions for the public school students.

From certain angles, you can see both the 1913 Woolworth Building and New York by Gehry seemingly side-by-side. The apposition of the two towers is important. Both represent the best of their ages—stylistically and technologically. There is nothing cookie-cutter about either building. Both are urban phenomena. Nooks and crannies exist in both—one through the use of Gothic niches and traditional ornament, the other through the wonderful pockets of space in the high-tech shifting steel.

What has not changed in the hundred years that separate the two buildings are the unsurpassed vistas that each building affords. New York is as photogenic and impressive today as it was a century ago.

The exterior of New York by Gehry showing the public school at its base.

Lower Manhattan: Beaux-Arts, Modernism, & Post-Modernism

Woolworth Building (see page 37)
233 Broadway (between Barclay Street and Park Place)

Old New York Times Building (see page 23)
41 Park Row (at Spruce Street)

New York by Gehry (see page 101)
8 Spruce Street (off Park Row)

    Subways
    A, C: Chamber Street Station
    2, 3: Park Place Station
    R: City Hall Station
    4, 5, 6: Brooklyn Bridge / City Hall Station
    J, Z: Fulton Street Station

    Buses
    M5: Park Place
    M22: City Hall
    M9, M103: Park Row

....

World Trade Center (see page 77)
Area bounded by Liberty, Church, Vesey, and West Streets

Equitable Building (see page 41)
120 Broadway (between Pine and Cedar Streets)

    Subways
    E: Word Trade Center Station
    4, 5: Fulton Street Station
    J, Z: Fulton Street Station

    Buses
    M5: Pine Street

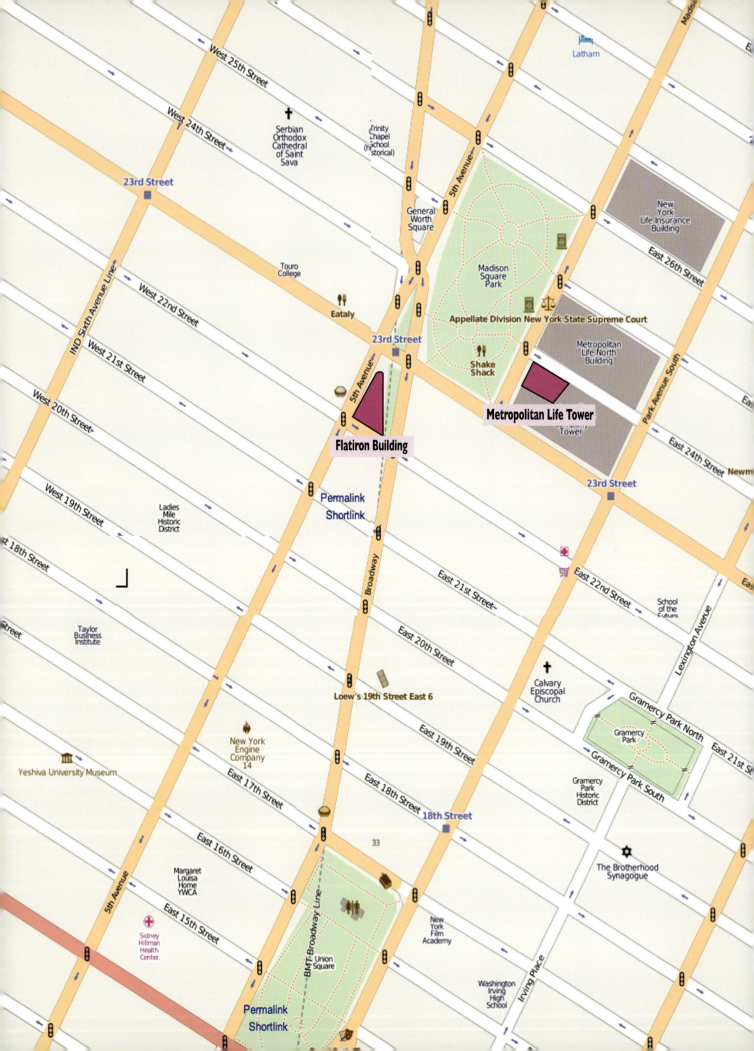

MADISON SQUARE: BEAUX-ARTS

Flatiron Building (see page 29)
175 Fifth Avenue (at 23rd Street)

Metropolitan Life Tower (see page 33)
1 Madison Avenue (at 23rd Street)

> Subways
> N, R: 23rd Street Station
> F, M: 23rd Street Station
> 6: 23rd Street Station
>
> Buses
> M1, M2, M3, M5: 23rd Street
> M23: Fifth Avenue

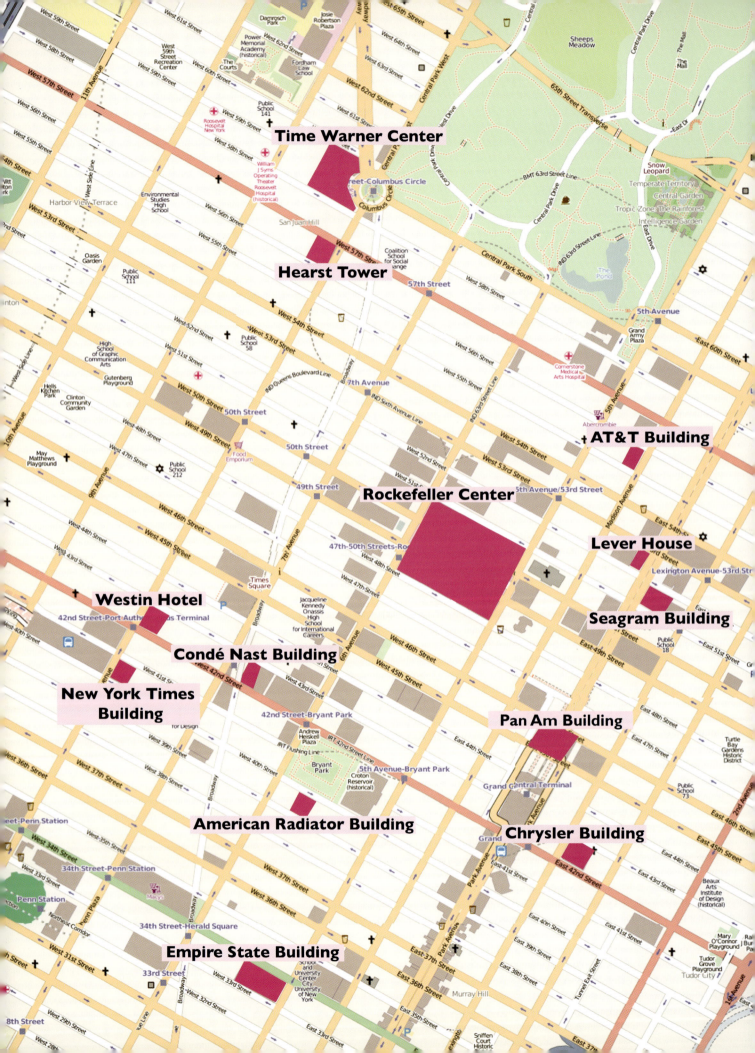

Midtown Manhattan: Art Deco, Modernism, & Post-Modernism

Empire State Building (see page 51)
350 Fifth Avenue (at 34th Street)

> Subways
> 1, 2, 3: 34th Street Station
> B, D, F, M, N, Q, R: Herald Square Station
> 6: 33rd Street Station
>
> Buses
> M1, M2, M3, M4, M5: 34th & 5th
> M34, M16: 5th Avenue

....

Chrysler Building (see page 47)
405 Lexington Avenue (at 42nd Street)

> Subways
> 4, 5, 6, 7, S - Grand Central Station
>
> Buses
> M1, M2, M3, M4: Madison Avenue & 42nd Street
> M42: Lexinton Avenue
> M101, M102, M103: 42nd Street

....

Westin Hotel (see page 89)
270 West 43rd Street (at Eighth Avenue)

New York Times Building (see page 99)
620 Eighth Avenue (between 40th and 41st Streets)

Condé Nast Building (see page 85)
4 Times Square (42nd Street and Broadway)

American Radiator Building (see page 43)
40 West 40th Street (between 5th and 6th Avenues)

> Subways
> A, C, E: 42nd Street / Port Authority Station
> 1, 2, 3, 7, N, Q, R: Times Square Station
> B, D, F, M: 42nd Street / Bryant Park Station
>
> Buses
> M7, M20: Times Square
> M16: Port Authority
> M42: Times Square or 8th Avenue
> M104: Times Square or 8th Avenue

Maps | 107

Rockefeller Center (see page 55)
48th to 52nd Streets between Fifth and Sixth Avenues

    Subways
    B, D, F, M: 47th-50th Streets / Rockefeller Center Station

    Buses
    M1, M2, M3, M4, M7: 49th Street Rockefeller Center
    M50: Avenue of the Americas or 5th Avenue

....

Lever House (see page 65)
390 Park Avenue (between 53rd and 54th Streets)

Seagram Building (see page 69)
375 Park Avenue (between 52nd and 53rd Streets)

AT&T Building (see page 81)
550 Madison Avenue (between 55th and 56th Streets)

    Subways
    E, M: 5th Avenue / 53rd Street Station
    6: 51st / Lexington Avenue Station

    Buses
    M1, M2, M3, M4, M101, M102, M103: 53rd or 55th Streets

....

Time Warner Center (see page 93)
10 Columbus Circle (59th Street & Broadway)

Hearst Tower (see page 95)
300 West 57th Street (at 8th Avenue)

    Subways
    A, B, C, D, 1: 59th Street / Columbus Circle Station

    Buses
    M7, M5, M10, M20, M104: 59th Street / Columbus Circle
    M31, M57: 8th Avenue

BIBLIOGRAPHY

Lynn S. Beedle, Mir M. Ali, and Paul J. Armstrong. *The Skyscraper and the City: Design, Technology, and Innovation.* Lewiston: Edwin Mellen Press, 2007.

Meredith L. Clausen. *The Pan Am Building and the Shattering of the Modernist Dream.* Cambridge, MA: MIT Press, 2005.

George H. Douglas. *Skyscrapers: A Social History of the Very Tall Building in America.* Jefferson, NC: McFarland & Co., 1996.

Benjamin S. Flowers. *Skyscraper: The Politics and Power of Building New York City in the Twentieth Century.* Philadelphia: University of Pennsylvania Press, 2009.

Paul Goldberger. *The Chippendale Skyscraper, and Other Curiosities of the Post-Modern Age of Architecture and Design.* New York: Times Books, 1983.

Paul Goldberger. *The Skyscraper.* New York: Alfred A. Knopf, 1992.

Elizabeth Hawes. *New York, New York: How the Apartment House Transformed the Life of the City (1869-1930).* New York: Knopf, 1993.

Ada Louise Huxtable. *The Tall Building Artistically Reconsidered: The Search for a Skyscraper Style.* Berkeley: University of California Press, 1992.

Charles Jencks. *The Iconic Building.* New York: Rizzoli, 2005.

Carol H. Krinsky. *Gordon Bunshaft of Skidmore, Owings & Merrill.* New York: Architectural History Foundation, 1988.

Sarah B. Landau and Carl W. Condit. *Rise of the New York Skyscraper, 1865-1913.* New Haven: Yale University Press, 1996.

Thomas A. P. Leeuwen. *The Skyward Trend of Thought: The Metaphysics of the American Skyscraper.* Cambridge, MA: MIT Press, 1988.

Caroline Mierop and Georges Binder. *Skyscrapers: Higher and Higher.* Paris: NORMA, 1995.

Roberta Moudry. *The American Skyscraper: Cultural Histories.* New York: Cambridge University Press, 2005.

Eric P. Nash. *New York's 50 Best Skyscrapers.* New York: City & Company, 1997.

Eric P. Nash and Norman McGrath. *Manhattan Skyscrapers.* New York: Princeton Architectural Press, 1999.

New York City Landmark Designation Reports, retrieved on-line at http://www.neighborhoodpreservationcenter.org/designation_reports.

Daniel Okrent. *Great Fortune: The Epic of Rockefeller Center.* New York: Viking, 2003.

Donald M. Reynolds. *The Architecture of New York City: Histories and Views of Important Structures, Sites and Symbols.* New York: Wiley, 1994.

Cervin Robinson and Rosemarie H. Bletter. *Skyscraper Style: Art Deco,* New York. New York: Oxford University Press, 1975.

Steven Ruttenbaum. *Mansions in the Clouds: The Skyscraper Palazzi of Emery Roth.* New York: Balsam Press, 1986.

Karl Sabbagh. *Skyscraper: The Making of a Building.* London: Macmillan, 1990.

Merrill Schleier. *The Skyscraper in American Art, 1890-1931.* Ann Arbor, MI: UMI Research Press, 1986.

Piera Scuri. *Late-twentieth-century Skyscrapers.* New York: Van Nostrand Reinhold, 1990.

Suzanne Stephens, Ian Luna, and Ron Broadhurst. *Imagining Ground Zero: Official and Unofficial Proposals for the World Trade Center Site.* New York: Rizzoli, 2004.

Robert A. M. Stern, Gregory Gilmartin, and Thomas Mellins. *New York 1930: Architecture and Urbanism between the Two World Wars.* New York: Rizzoli, 1987.

Robert A. M. Stern. *New York 1900: Metropolitan Architecture and Urbanism, 1890-1915.* New York: Rizzoli, 1995.

Robert A. M. Stern, David Fishman, and Thomas Mellins. *New York 1960.* New York, NY: Monacelli Press, 1997.

Robert A. M. Stern, David Fishman, and Jacob Tilove. *New York 2000: Architecture and Urbanism between the Bicentennial and the Millennium.* New York: Monacelli Press, 2006.

Robert A. M. Stern, David Fishman, and Thomas Mellins. *New York 1880: Architecture and Urbanism in the Gilded Age.* New York: Monacelli Press, 2009.

John Tauranac. *The Empire State Building: The Making of a Landmark.* New York: Scribner, 1995.

Susan Tunick. *Terra Cotta-Don't Take It for Granite: 3 Walks in New York City Neighborhoods.* New York: Friends of Terra Cotta Press, 1995.

Susan Tunick, and Peter Mauss. *Terra-cotta Skyline: New York's Architectural Ornament.* New York: Princeton Architectural Press, 1997.

Schaik L. Van, Hamzah Razaleigh, and Ken Yeang. *Vertical Ecoinfrastructure: Work of T.R. Hamzah & Yeang.* Mulgrave, Vic: Images, 2009.

Matthew Wells. *Skyscrapers: Structure and Design.* New Haven, CT: Yale University Press, 2005.

Carol Willis. *Form Follows Finance: Skyscrapers and Skylines in New York and Chicago.* New York: Princeton Architectural Press, 1995.

Carol Willis and Donald Friedman. *Building the Empire State.* New York: W.W. Norton in association with the Skyscraper Museum, 1998.

Ken Yeang. *The Green Skyscraper: The Basis for Designing Sustainable Intensive Buildings.* Munich: Prestel, 1999.

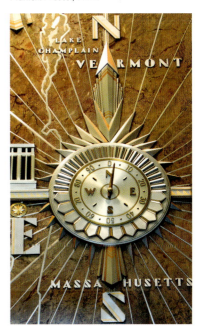

Photo Credits
All photos are by the author except as noted. Berenice Abbott/WPA, 77; Beinecke Rare Book and Manuscript Library, Yale University, 14; Ryan Browne, Cook+Fox Architects, 7; Enselado, 19; Jeffmock, CC-BY-SA-3.0, 76; Imelenchon, 29; Library of Congress 10, 12, 15, 17, 23, 24, 25, 29, 35, 41, 51, 73, 75, 77, New York Tribune, 13; © OpenStreetMap contributors, CC-BY-SA, 102 104 106; PAT M IN NYC, 38; Patrick Ramade, 9; Postdlf, 72; Leonard Ross, 2, 110; David Shankbone, 83; Smurfy, CC-BY-SA-3.0-MIGRATED, 78; Anatoly Terentiev, 33; U.S. Patent Office, 18.

Dr. Seth Gopin was born in New York City and although he was raised and worked in New Jersey for most of his life, he is once again a resident of Manhattan. He earned a BA in French from Rutgers College (1979) and a Ph.D. in Art History from Rutgers University (1994). He served in the U.S. Army for four years as a Russian linguist, and was employed at Rutgers for more than a quarter of a century in a variety of administrative posts. He oversaw the Office for Scholarships and Fellowships, was in charge of Study Abroad Programs, and served as the Director of Global Studies. In addition, he was a popular lecturer in art history. In 2006 he retired from Rutgers but has remained quite active. He was editor of *News Tibet*, the north American newsletter for the Tibetan Government-in-Exile and, most recently, has been a regular lecturer on Cunard ships.

Dr. Gopin's scholarly interests have focused on two principal areas. He is a specialist in exoticism in eighteenth-century European art, and has published extensively on the Franco-Flemish painter Jean Baptiste Vanmour, who worked in Constantinople. He is also very much interested in urban architecture and the structure of cities, and has taught in Paris and New York. He is a Chevalier of the Ordre des Palmes Académiques.

Metro Insights, LLC
Metro Insights is a small, private company founded in 2007 by two art historians. It offers bespoke tours of London, Paris, and New York, with an emphasis on the art, culture, and life of these three vibrant cities. This book is the first of a series of publications Metro Insights plans to issue, and it will soon be offering architectural and related studies on its website at: www.metroinsights.com.